INDIA IN YOUR POCKET

INDIA
IN YOUR POCKET

A STEP-BY-STEP GUIDE
AND TRAVEL ITINERARY

**BY ANURAG MATHUR
WITH LEELA KANUGA &
SUMITA PAUL**

Horizon Books

British Library Cataloguing in Publication Data

Mathur, Anurag
  India in your pocket: a step-by-step
  guide and travel itinerary — Pocket
  travellers
  1. India (Republic) — Visitors' guides
  I. Title II. Series
  915.4′0452

  ISBN 1-85461-015-5

© 1988 by Anurag Mathur
UK edition © 1989 by Horizon Books Ltd

Maps Jim Wood

This edition first published in 1989 by Horizon Books Ltd, Harper & Row House, Estover Road, Plymouth PL6 7PZ, United Kingdom. Tel: Plymouth (0752) 705251. Telex: 45635. Fax: (0752) 777603.

Printed in Great Britain by BPCC Wheatons Ltd, Exeter

CONTENTS

HOW TO USE THIS BOOK

Namaste. Literally translated it means, 'I salute the divine in you,' but as I overheard one teenager tell another, 'It means "Hi" in Hindi.'

This book attempts what many have assured me is impossible: to take you around India in a short space of time and still give you a feel of the major cities, important tourist spots, dramatically different regions, as well as some of the lesser known but interesting places. Obviously, the only way to get around a land mass this size is by air, and *India in Your Pocket* tells you how to get the most out of Indian Airlines' budget priced Discover India fare. I also tell you where to find the most interesting restaurants and accommodation along the way in all price ranges from extravagant to ridiculously inexpensive.

India in Your Pocket gives you the travel efficiency of an organised tour plus do-it-yourself freedom and flexibility. It presents what I personally consider to be an ideal plan for touring India—but I'm not you. Modify the plan to suit your schedule and interests. If you want to see a place that's not on the itinerary, rearrange the itinerary. However, do remember that Indian Airlines is less than dazzling in coping with sudden changes. If you have a Discover India fare you'll have to book again though you are not charged for a 'no-show'. If you have a point-to-point ticket, a percentage of the ticket value is deducted depending on how late you cancel.

The itinerary format used in this book is divided into sections, each containing:

1. A **suggested schedule** for travel, sightseeing, shopping and meals.
2. An **orientation** to each city you'll visit.
3. **Transport** information telling you how to get to each destination, how to get around once you're there and how much to pay.
4. Major **sightseeing highlights.** These are rated in order of importance: ▲▲▲ Don't miss; ▲▲ Try hard to see; and ▲ See if you get a chance.
5. **Lodging** and **food** recommendations to help you get the most for your money, with special emphasis on regional cuisines.
6. **Maps** showing how to get to the places discussed in the text.

When To Go

Some places such as Rajasthan, which are largely desert, are best seen in winter because in summer the place is a furnace.

Kashmir, cradled by mountains, is at its beautiful best in summer and autumn. By and large, autumn and winter are the best times to visit the country and avoid extreme heat. I have included Tours 18, 19 and 20 in Rajasthan on the assumption that you'll be visiting between October 15 and March 15. If you're going to India at another time of year, substitute the Kashmir option for these days.

The monsoons are usually from June to August. There are torrential rains, and it's best not to fly within India during monsoon season since air connections become erratic.

Clothing

Plan your wardrobe according to the season of your visit. In winter, two sweaters (one light and one heavy) as well as an anorak or jacket are necessary, especially in north India where temperatures vary widely between day and night. In the south, light clothing will be adequate. Bring comfortable footwear—trainers for winter or flat sandals for summer.

It's a chauvinist's country. Men can wear anything, or almost nothing, and not have an eyebrow raised. Women wearing shorts or short skirts are regarded as immodest, particularly in smaller towns. Women are therefore advised to keep their legs covered. Bare female legs seem to galvanize the hormones of the most sedate males into hysterical activity.

Entering India

There are rules for everything, which most Indians not only ignore but are often not even aware of. When entering and leaving India remember the following and you'll be okay:

■ Register the amount of money you're bringing in so you can take it out again.

■ As far as possible avoid bringing in or taking out gold in any form. The customs people are fiends about this.

■ Don't get caught with any kind of drugs at customs. An Indian jail makes *Midnight Express* look like a luxury resort.

■ You'll have to pay your hotel bills in foreign exchange, whether as cash or travellers' cheques, so keep your sterling handy. However, the smaller hotels can only accept rupees; ask when checking in.

■ Remember when shopping, **the export from India of antiquities and art objects more than 100 years old is prohibited.**

■ For complete details on import and export regulations (which are quite complex) contact the nearest Government of India Tourist Office.

If you've fallen in love with India and plan to stay more than three months, a Registration Certificate and Residential Permit should be obtained from the nearest Foreigners' Registration Office within seven days of your arrival. Your personal appearance is absolutely necessary at the time of registration, extension or exit. Four photographs are also required for registration. Foreigners registered at the Foreigners' Registration Office are required to report any change of address, and also must inform the Registration Office regarding their absence for more than fifteen days.

Indian Airlines

Indian Airlines offer two incentive schemes for air travel within India. The Discover India fare costs about £150 and must be paid in foreign currency. It allows 21 days' travel within the country provided no city is touched more than once except for the purpose of transfers or connections. The India Wonderfare (about £100) permits unlimited travel for one week within any of four regions—north, south, east and west. It gives year-round economy class travel between cities in the region of your choice provided you don't touch the same point more than once except for the purpose of transfers and connections.

Hotels

We suggest you do your bookings well in advance, at least two months ahead. During the peak season, October to March, most hotels get full very quickly, especially in Delhi.

Put your valuables in the safe deposit locker at the hotel or guest house in which you're staying. Remember to get a receipt.

There is a 10% surcharge on room rent and all food and beverages consumed in a hotel. Remember to add that to your calculations or you may be in for a rude surprise.

At some point, if you're in India during the summer, you'll discover the subtle difference between a room that is air conditioned and one that is air cooled. The former is cooled by the usual system, while the latter is refrigerated by an object the size, shape and colour of a bear, which emits a blast of air that will pin you to the wall. But it's welcome in the summer. If the blast turns hot, inform the receptionist that the water pump that cools the beast has run down again.

Before you check into any hotel in India, I urge you to confirm that it has a 'Western-style bathroom', that is, one that contains your familiar, friendly toilet. The alternative is the Indian-style toilet, which is slit trench with tiles. While this method of relieving yourself is believed to be excellent (the human race used this method exclusively in earlier times), modern man's knees are such that once you sit down, unless you're a trained athlete, you may be unable to get up again. There isn't (I am told) much romance to be found while squatting in a bathroom for the duration of your stay.

Money

The Indian rupee (Rs) consists of 100 units, called paise. Coins are in denominations of five, ten, twenty, twenty-five and fifty paise, as well as one and two rupees. It's wisest to exchange your money through authorised banks and money changers while in India, and remember to keep the receipts. (This will enable you to reconvert the money when you depart from India.) The informal tourist network may suggest various helpful gentlemen in dark corners who will offer you "black market" rates, but the rewards aren't worth the risks.

It's best to carry only as much money as you need and change your travellers' cheques only as required. Many of the larger shops and hotels, particularly in bigger towns, accept travellers' cheques and credit cards.

Tipping: Taxi and auto rickshaw drivers are not tipped, waiters are. 10% of your bill is sufficient. There are the other normal blights on a traveller's life such as doormen and porters—tip them if you're in a good mood.

Beggars: They regard tourists as God's gift, have whining voices like electric drills and a persistence which, if put to better use, could probably get them elected to parliament. Learn to roll up your windows with agility and gaze with passionate intensity into the distance. When provoked, scream. Initially you feel sorry for them and pay up, but you'll be amazed at how quickly you learn to ignore them. If you tip one, hordes of his colleagues will materialise from nowhere, believing they've found one of the type born every minute.

Haggling: There are, unfortunately, no hard and fast rules. Don't bother haggling in government shops, or for merchandise with the price printed on it. However, merchants in makeshift stalls are likely to offer prices in direct proportion to how affluent you look. It's best to walk through a couple of shops comparing prices, ideally with a look of disbelief on your face throughout. Shopping in India is the best training available for an acting career.

Food and Health Precautions

Before leaving, we would advise that you get an anti-cholera and typhoid injection. You should carry anti-malarial tablets, analgesics, anti-emetic and anti-diarrheal tablets. Antihistamines if you suffer from allergies, as well as a broad-spectrum antibiotic to take care of minor infections, should complete the list. And, of course, things like plasters, antiseptic cream and water purification tablets should also be part of your medical kit. Anti-mosquito coils to light at night can prove very useful. These can be bought in India.

'Delhi Belly' is a common stomach problem faced by many who visit India. It can happen anywhere, not just in the capital. However, if you're reasonably careful about your food and drink, you should not face problems. Carry water purification tablets or drink the bottled mineral water, failing which, drink boiled water or carbonated drinks such as Campa, Thums Up or Limca. Check with your hotel to find out whether they treat the water. It's not that the water is always foul—after all, 700 million Indians drink it every day of their lives and live to a jolly old age—it's mostly that the bacteria in the water are very different from those found in the water of other countries. If it's any consolation, the first time I went to the U.S.A. I was racked with cramps for three days.

Avoid open and cut food and unclean eating corners, especially those exposed to flies. The shopkeeper will simply blow the flies away and assure you that his wares are now perfectly clean. Or that his flies are legendary for their exquisite hygienic habits. But it's best avoided.

Do sample Indian food; just be sensible. Don't eat off the roadside, and choose a clean-looking restaurant. Check that the food isn't too spicy, though oddly some westerners eat chillies in quantities that would slay Indians.

Sometimes toilet paper is available, sometimes (particularly when you need it most) not. The reason is that the locals use water instead of tissue. For the same reason, the left hand is regarded as unclean and the right hand is used to offer and exchange gifts and to eat with. Toilet paper is easily purchasable in almost all grocery shops.

You might be tempted to eat with your hands like other Indians. It takes quite a lot of practice—but don't give up, and remember to use only your right hand.

In case of health emergencies, there are two types of hospitals—government and private. The government hospitals are usually very large and crowded, but they are cheap and have a full complement of doctors. The private hospitals are more specialised, much more comfortable and far more expensive. Your hotel can direct you if necessary.

Communications

Radio and television are state owned and regarded as channels for entertainment. Objective news is still obtained largely from the newspapers and magazines, which are almost always privately owned. However the Indian press, like most Indians, has very little interest in the outside world, and after a few weeks you may be a noted authority on one of the numerous local scandals while you wouldn't know if your own country had sunk under the sea. The Indian press is completely free, vociferously opinionated and highly credible.

The Indian postal service is good. Letters within the country must have a Rs .60 stamp for the first 100 grammes and another Rs .40 for every additional 10 grammes. For foreign destinations use an aerogramme (Rs 5). Foreign airmail letters usually require stamps of Rs 6.50 or more depending on their destination. Domestic telegrams up to 10 words cost Rs 3.50 and every additional word costs 50 paisa. Express (extra fast service) telegrams cost exactly double. Foreign telegrams are of two categories: ordinary at a minimum rate of Rs 2.50 per word and LT (Letter Telegram) that takes longer but costs exactly half. Telexes can be sent from some post offices. Long distance calls can either be booked or dialled direct within India (STD) or internationally (ISTD). Ask your hotel desk for details.

Recommended guidebooks

India: Travel Survival Kit, Lonely Planet Publications. *Fodor's India, Nepal and Sri Lanka,* Fodor's Guides. *Asia Through the Back Door* by Rick Steves and John Gottberg, available from Horizon Books.

WELCOME TO INDIA

Nothing quite prepares you for India—the world's highest mountain range, endless miles of desert, luxuriant forests, magnificent beaches, wildlife, a history and culture that go back four thousand years. India is 3000 miles from north to south and has a population of 700 million people who speak one or more of 18 major languages and over a thousand dialects. The variety of arts, crafts and cuisine is dazzling. Though a poor country, India is one of the ten most industrialised nations in the world. It has hundreds of millions of illiterates as well as the world's third largest pool of trained engineers and scientists. The GNP is low, but the nation is self-sufficient in food, exports grains, manufactures everything it needs from needles to trains, pins to battleships, even nuclear power stations and satellites which it has placed in orbit with its own rockets.

India can create culture shock. Don't expect it to be an extension of Europe. India is alien and completely different. You see people all the time and everywhere. They are loud, spontaneous, warm, friendly and often inquisitive. Indians are almost universally friendly toward Westerners, but may become excessively personal. Questions about your job, financial status, family and marital situation, as well as heated debates among listeners about any or all of these, can be quite common.

With the current emphasis on tourism (India gets over a million tourists a year) India has developed an efficient tourist infrastructure. If this is your first visit, it is advisable that you stick to the well-travelled circuits and not be too adventurous. The reactions of visitors are often extreme. Many adore the land, others detest it. No one is indifferent to it.

India is a shopper's bargain paradise, with an incredible variety of exquisite handicrafts at amazingly low prices. Brassware, carved wood, bone and ivory, carpets, textiles, jewellery and silks, plain or with heavy brocade. Your budget and your baggage space should be planned accordingly.

The bureaucracy is beastly. If it's any consolation, it's not just to visitors. It's worse towards Indians. Other than that, the people are warm and friendly. Not only friendly, they create relationships at first glance. You'll get used to children toddling up and addressing you as 'Uncle' or 'Auntie' (usually pronounced 'ankle' and 'NT').

India is not as conservative a country as most foreigners believe. Public displays of affection, however, are almost unknown between people of different sexes, though men walking hand in hand and hugging each other is quite common. They're not gay, they're just (as the film stars say) good friends. While Indian men welcome a handshake, Indian women shy away from any physical contact with a man. The *namaste* (greeting with hands folded in prayer position) is safe and will be highly appreciated.

There are also some religious norms that have to be followed. For instance, while visiting Sikh shrines, it's obligatory to cover your head. You can use your handkerchief. It is the norm, though not obligatory, in Hindu temples as well. Here, remember to remove your shoes before entering. Clothing should be modest when visiting holy shrines.

India is a completely free country, and one of the greatest joys for Indians is to abuse their government and despair at how badly India is doing. They're also, at the same time, very patriotic, so it isn't a good idea for you as a foreigner to agree with them. If, on the other hand, you tactfully offer some kind words about the country, in all probability Indians will not only beam upon you but also press into your shrinking palm some insufferably oily sweets.

Religion

India is the usually tolerant host to virtually every religion on earth. There is Hinduism — complex, subtle, ancient beyond reckoning, confusing in its myriad gods and goddesses. It believes, in essence, that a single life force permeates the entire universe and that all things are manifestations of this life force. Hence the emphasis on vegetarianism. It believes in *dharma* (duty) and *karma* (that our place in this life is determined by our actions in our previous lives, just as our actions in this one will determine our next rebirth). Thousands of sects, numbering about 500 million people, comprise what is generically called Hinduism.

There are also 90 million Muslims, and 15 million Christians some of whom trace their arrival in India to St. Thomas, he who doubted. There are 14 million Sikhs, a handful of Zoroastrians (called Parsis) who worship fire, and tribals who follow a primitive animism. There even exists a small, flourishing Jewish community, though now most have emigrated to Israel.

All religions are respected, and for thousands of years people have come to India seeking enlightenment. Many find teachers who provide insights and perhaps solace; many others find charlatans who see themselves purely as profitable businesses set up by the wayside to fleece travellers on the road of spiritual quest.

True, there is great spirituality in the land, but there is also appalling cruelty. Sometimes I think one can't say a single thing about India without finding the opposite to be equally true.

ITINERARY

NOTE: Unless otherwise mentioned, all travel is by Indian Airlines daily flights. The flight schedules change frequently, and this itinerary should be used only as a guide. Please confirm flight timings before planning your itinerary.

TOUR 1 Arrive at Delhi's Indira Gandhi International Airport. Get a prepaid taxi to the city (about 30 minutes' drive). Check into any one of the many good hotels in Delhi. Morning free for rest and recovery from jet-lag. The afternoon can be used for sightseeing. Visit parts of Old Delhi, the Red Fort and the Jama Masjid, India's largest mosque. Both structures were built by the 17th century Mughal Emperor Shah Jahan. From here, move on to Connaught Circus, a shopping and business centre in the heart of New Delhi. Evening free for rest or perhaps a cultural programme.

TOUR 2 Full day in Delhi. This day can be utilised for shopping and visiting other places of tourist interest like the Qutab Minar, considered the world's most perfect specimen of tower architecture; Hauz Khas, named after the great reservoir *(hauz)* built in 1305 by early Muslim ruler Alauddin Khiji; Humayun's Tomb; the Jantar Mantar Observatory; the tombs of the Lodhi kings; the Purana Quila (old fort) and the adjacent zoo. India Tourism Development Corporation (ITDC) and Delhi Tourism run conducted tours of the city. In the evening, see an open-air sound-and-light programme at the Red Fort (two shows, one of them in English, every evening except during the July and August monsoon season).

TOUR 3 Leave Delhi for Jaipur—the 'Pink City' of India, so called because most of the buildings are made of red sandstone (departure 06:40, arrival 07:15). Drive to the city (about 20 minutes). After check-in and breakfast, visit the Amber Fort, the last stretch of which is an ascent on foot or by elephant. Return to the hotel for lunch. In the afternoon, visit the Observatory built by Maharaja Jai Singh, the founder of Jaipur. Drive past the Hawa Mahal (Palace of Winds) and visit the City Museum. Evening free for shopping.

TOUR 4 After an early breakfast, leave for Agra (150 km) by car or coach. On the way, visit Fatehpur Sikri, the Mughal capital in 1559. Reach Agra by lunchtime. In the afternoon, visit the Taj Mahal and the Agra Fort. Evening free.

TOUR 5 Leave Agra for Khajuraho (departure 08:30, arrival 09:10), famous for its sculpted and ornamental temples. The excellent carvings display a love of life, a playful spontaneity. Lovers in various postures of amorous delight are portrayed in minute detail. The sculptures are sensuous and erotic. Processions, animals, the entire panorama of life is shown. Of the original 85 temples, only 22 remain today. They are spread over an area of 10 square kilometres. Visit the museum adjacent to the temples. Evening free.

TOUR 6 Leave Khajuraho for Varanasi (departure 09:40, arrival 10:20). Varanasi, also called Benares, is probably the oldest continuously inhabited city in the world. Morning free for check-in and rest. After lunch visit Sarnath, 10 km away. Sarnath, an important Buddhist site, is where Buddha preached his first sermon. Visit the stupa, a commemorative monument, and the museum. On the return drive visit the Benares Hindu University, the largest residential university in Asia. Evening free. Try to attend a local theatre or a music concert.

TOUR 7 Set out before dawn to the riverside. The ghats (steps leading down to the river from a steep bank) at sunrise are a must. Go for an early morning boat ride on the river Ganga. Observe the ancient and time-honoured rituals being practised. Some of these are fascinating, others repelling. Avoid Manikarnika ghat (though that's where your boatman would love to take you). It is the burning ghat and has several cremations at a time. Photography at Manikarnika is strictly prohibited. Visit the famed Vishwanath Temple (the Golden Temple), so called because of the gold plating on the towers. Spend the rest of the morning walking through the streets and shopping, especially for silks and carpets. In the afternoon, take in more sights like the Durga Kund Temple, the Bharat Mata Temple, the Sankat Mochan Temple (the monkey temple) and the temple of Kal Bhairav (a primitive, awe-inspiring deity). Evening free. Take a rickshaw ride and travel the way Benaresis do.

TOUR 8 In the morning, take a boat ride across the Ganga to visit the Ramnagar Fort and Museum, which boasts a wonderful collection of art objects. Afternoon free for shopping. Leave Varanasi for Calcutta (departure 19:30, arrival 20:40). Check in at a city hotel.

TOUR 9 Spend the morning exploring Calcutta, founded in 1690 and today one of the world's largest cities. Visit the Victoria Memorial, India's tribute to Queen Victoria, as well as the Indian Museum and various bazaars. For lunch, try one of the

restaurants in Park Street, a favourite haunt of the elite in
Calcutta.

Leave Calcutta for Madras (departure 17:30, arrival 19:35).
Check into your hotel and rest for the night.

TOUR 10 The highlight of a visit to Madras is a one-day
excursion by car to Mahaballipuram and Kanchipuram (100 km).
The rock sculptures of Mahaballipuram display a perfection of
technique, and the Shore Temple is worth a visit. Kanchipuram,
once the city of a thousand temples, still contains about 124 rock-
cut shrines.

TOUR 11 Leave Madras for Trivandrum (departure 06:35,
arrival 08:35). Trivandrum is the capital of Kerala, a state with
India's highest literacy rate and lush, green countryside. Catch a
bus from the city to Cape Comorin (85 km), the southernmost tip
of India, a point where three oceans—the Bay of Bengal, the
Arabian Sea and the Indian Ocean—meet.

TOUR 12 If it happens to be a Monday, your flight is at 12:30
so you have time to go down to Kovalum Beach (13 km) or go
around the city with its generous sprinkling of churches, mosques
and temples juxtaposed with modern buildings.

If your flight is on any other day of the week, you'll have to
forego this, as the departure time is 09:10. You arrive in Goa at
13:55 (Monday) or 11:20 (other days). After lunch, visit the
popular Calangute Beach. In the evening take a stroll through the
city.

TOUR 13 Join the South Goa conducted tour and have your fill
of the splendid, lavishly ornamented Latin churches. In the
evening take a river cruise and join in the dance and music.

TOUR 14 Leave Goa for Bombay (departure 13:00, arrival
13:55). Transfer to hotel. Walk around and spend time observing
the most Westernised city of India and one of Asia's busiest
seaports. Bombay has an active theatre culture. Spend the evening
watching a play or a cultural programme. Take a drive to
Malabar Hill and look down at the well-lit Marine Drive,
popularly known as the 'Queen's Necklace'.

TOUR 15 Bombay, known as the Hollywood of India because of
its cinema industry, is the capital of Maharashtra state. Places
worth visiting include the Prince of Wales Museum, the Hanging
Gardens and the Gateway of India, a commemorative structure
resembling the Arc de Triomphe. Keep half a day free to visit the
famous Elephanta Caves across Bombay Harbour. Evening free.

Check at the hotel for information about local programmes.

TOUR 16 Leave Bombay for Aurangabad (departure 06:15, arrival 06:55). After check-in and breakfast at the hotel, take a packed lunch and leave by car or coach for Ellora, 28 km away. The sculpted cave temples of Ellora are the product of three religious systems—Buddhism, Brahminism and Jainism. On the way back, visit the medieval fortress at Daulatabad, which was the capital of India for a short while in the 12th century. Late afternoon/evening for sightseeing at Aurangabad, depending on how tired or fit you feel. Visit the Mughal Emperor Aurangzeb's grave and Bibi ka Makbara, a mausoleum built in 1679 by Aurangzeb for his wife Rabia-ud-Daurabi.

TOUR 17 Leave early morning and drive to the Ajanta Caves (104 km), which date back to the 2nd century BC and are famous for their excellent frescoes.

TOUR 18 Leave Aurangabad for Udaipur (departure 07:25, arrival 08:30), founded in 1559 by Maharana Udai Singh. Udaipur is a city of palaces and lakes. Some of the palaces have been turned into luxurious five-star hotels. Visit the Royal Palace, now a museum. Your hotel is likely to have a Rajasthani folk dance performance every evening. If so, don't miss it.

TOUR 19 Leave Udaipur for Jodhpur (departure 08:55, arrival 09:25). As you're not spending the night here, it may be a good idea to drive straight to the railway station and check your baggage into the cloakroom. Get set to see Jodhpur, a city surrounded by an immense wall which separates it from the desert sands that stretch out on all sides. Visit the massive fortress in the morning. In the afternoon, visit the temples and the old buildings in the city. After dinner, drive to the railway station and take the overnight train to Jaisalmer (departure 22:15, arrival 07:30).

TOUR 20 The ancient city of Jaisalmer, founded by Rawal Jaisal in 1156, lies in the heart of the Thar, the great Indian desert. Within are temples, forts and palaces built of yellow sandstone. Overlooking the city is the fort—famous for its Jain temples and library containing ancient manuscripts. Take the overnight train back to Jodhpur (departure 20:10, arrival 06:30).

LEAVING INDIA Drive straight to the airport for the flight to Delhi (departure 09:50, arrival 11:35). Evening/night—catch your flight home.

OPTION: KASHMIR
(March 15-October 15)

TOUR 17 Leave Aurangabad for Delhi (departure 07:25, arrival 11:35). Visit the city for more shopping and the sightseeing you have missed. Check your homeward flight booking.

TOUR 18 Leave Delhi for Srinagar (departure 09:00, arrival 10:15). You've probably had enough of hotels, so why not hire a houseboat on the Dal or Nagin Lakes. Go to the Tourist Reception Centre for bookings and enquiries about excursions. Take a boat trip and watch the sun set over the lake. The evening can be kept free for relaxation.

TOUR 19 Take a day excursion tour to one of the many places around Srinagar. You could go to Sonemarg (the meadow of gold), Verinag with its beautiful spring, Gulmarg (the meadow of flowers), Martand (site of an ancient sun temple), Kokarnag or Yusmarg (both beautiful hill towns). Evening—relax and soothe those tired muscles.

TOUR 20 Morning—Srinagar sightseeing: see the Chashmashahi, the Dal and Nagin Lakes, Hazratbal and the famed Shalimar and Nishat gardens. En route, shop for Kashmiri handicrafts—shawls, carpets and papier mache articles. Leave for the airport for your flight to Delhi (departure 11:05, arrival 12:20). Catch your flight back home.

TOUR 1

ARRIVAL IN DELHI

For some mysterious reason, all international flights to India arrive at ungodly hours of the night. Your flight will arrive at the Indira Gandhi International Airport, 21 km from the city. Your first stop is the Immigration counter, and you should be through within half an hour. There are several counters at the Customs area. Customs officers are generally pleasant unless harassed, and clearance is merely a formality. There are two channels, green and red. If you have nothing to declare, which is probable, go through the green channel. At the baggage claim area, your baggage should be cleared in 20 minutes at the outside. Trolleys are parked alongside for your use. Free porters are available, though they frequently and fiercely dispute the 'free' part. Exchange sterling for rupees at the 24 hour airport bank, which offers the official exchange rate.

The arrival lounge has a duty free shop. Nearby are several tourist assistance counters. The Government of India's Tourist Counter is for information. The officers understand new arrivals' anxieties about India. Don't hesitate to ask questions that may seem obvious or naive. They'll even tell you about snake charmers (who still exist, today thanks largely to tourists).

The Ashok Travels and Tours counter does bookings in their India Tourism Development Corporation (ITDC) chain of hotels. The government-owned chain, the largest in India, offers a wide budget range. Ashok also organises various package tours, and you can hire a chauffeur-driven car from them if you wish.

The Travel Agents Association of India counter will provide information about the various travel agencies in India, the tours they organise and the services they offer.

There is also a counter for rail bookings to any part of the country. The booking and reservation system is computerised and you will be issued with a small sheet of paper, much like a cheque, which is both your reservation and your ticket. Guard it with your life. If you lose it you will have to make difficult and lengthy explanations to the railway officials, buy a new ticket and apply for a refund.

For transport into the city, both taxis and coaches have prepaid fare counters.Prominently displayed at the taxi counter is a list of fares to various locations, so you know exactly how much you'll have to pay. All taxis operating from the counter are registered, so it's a good idea to hire a taxi there. If the driver attempts to exercise what taxi drivers around the world regard as a divine right — that of fleecing tourists — you can phone 3014896 and complain. Between 23:00 and 05:00, 25% extra is charged above the metered fare. Baggage charges are Rs 2 per piece. Tipping is optional, though it may be hard to resist the driver's histrionic pleas. Tip him Rs 10 at most and ignore his look of contempt.

The coach is much cheaper. It goes past the Ashoka, Maurya, Taj Palace, Hyatt, Claridges and Janpath hotels, stopping finally at Connaught Place, the centre of New Delhi. Check the location of the hotel you want to reach with the Tourist Information Centre, and if your destination falls midway between stops just let the driver know. He'll stop the coach so you can get off, a noble gesture no other bus driver in your visit to India is likely to repeat.

Suggested Schedule

Early Morning	Arrive and check into hotel. Rest until lunch.
13:00	Visit the Jama Masjid.
14:30	Visit the Red Fort.
16:30	Visit Connaught Place, Cottage Industries Emporium and the Tourist Office. Shopping.
18:30	Return to hotel for dinner and rest or see a cultural show (the newspapers carry daily listings, or ask at the India Tourist Office in Janpath).

Delhi

Delhi, the capital of India, blends past and present vividly. The city has seen the rise and fall of so many dynasties that reference has often been made to the 'seven cities of Delhi'. Legend has it that Delhi was founded as early as 1200 BC by the Pandavas, heroes of the Indian religious epic, the *Mahabharata*. History is everywhere, and the past is always present. The altitude of Delhi is 239 metres above sea level, and the city's population is 6.87 million. Common languages are Hindi, English, Punjabi.

The city is divided into Old and New Delhi, and each has its distinct character. Old Delhi's streets are crowded even by Indian standards (and that's quite a crowd), but it is vibrant with smells and colours, and many historic monuments. New Delhi is more spacious and orderly. It was planned by British architects and planners in the early 20th century when the capital was moved from Calcutta. Connaught Place and Janpath, the city's main shopping and business areas, are situated here. Most of the best hotels are also in the southern part of New Delhi.

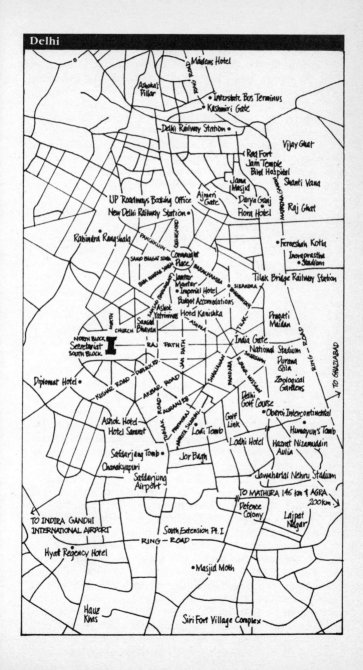

Delhi

The Cottage Industries Emporium is an ideal place to shop for handicrafts from all parts of the country. The variety is incredible and there are items in all price ranges. Nowhere else in India will you find such a wide selection of goods with assured quality. The prices are fixed, so don't bargain. (Shopping in Janpath, however, you are expected to haggle fiercely.)

Janpath is a very long road, but to Delhi-ites the name refers specifically to the crowded shopping area around and opposite the Tourist Office. Shops sell handicrafts, curios and antiques as well as garments. While the Cottage Industries Emporium remains your best bet for handicrafts, Janpath's ready-to-wear cotton casuals and more expensive silks are worth buying. Try several shops before making your purchases.

Most offices and commercial establishments are open Monday to Friday. While Connaught Place, the main shopping area, closes on Sunday, other shopping areas close on different days of the week. Larger shops close for lunch between 13:00 and 15:00. Museums close on different days — check before going.

A city map is essential. Get one from the Tourist Office at Janpath, where you can also book the city sightseeing tour.

Transport

Avoid buses, as they are so overcrowded you have to be an olympic class athlete to get on and off. Taxis and three-wheeler auto rickshaws have metered fares. Occasionally the fares are revised by the government and at such times the drivers are supposed to charge the rates stipulated on a card they carry. Between 23:00 and 06:00 there is a 25% surcharge on the metered fare.

You can take the regular afternoon guided tour offered by Delhi Tourism to Red Fort, Raj Ghat, Shantivan and Jama Masjid. Sightseeing on your own is definitely more interesting.

Sightseeing Highlights

▲▲▲**Jama Masjid** — An eloquent reminder of Mughal religious fervour, India's largest mosque was built by Shah Jahan in 1656 at the height of Mughal power. The mosque stands opposite the Red Fort. There is not very much to see within, but the building with its onion-shaped domes is a good example of Mughal architecture. Take off your shoes before entering. You can ascend the two minarets on payment of Rs 2 and get a magnificent view. The road to the mosque, crowded and loud, will test your enthusiasm to see the sight.

▲▲▲**The Red Fort** — The impressive Red Fort stands along the eastern edge of the walled city (Old Delhi) on the west bank of the River Yamuna. The Red Fort was built as a royal residence by the Mughal Emperor Shah Jahan. Direct public buses connect the Regal bus stop at Connaught Place to the Red Fort. A scooter, costing around Rs 10, is quicker. A cheaper mode (Rs 2.50 per person) is a point-to-point four-seater — a powerful, magnificently noisy converted Harley Davidson motorcycle. Buy an inexpensive guidebook, available outside the fort, and go through the area yourself.

Entry is through the Lahore Gate (so named because it faces Lahore, about 500 miles away). Inside are the Diwan-i-Am (Hall of Public Audience) and the Diwan-i-Khas (Hall of Private Audience), a luxurious chamber where the king would hold private meetings while seated on his solid gold peacock throne (now in Tehran). Then visit the Royal Baths and the Moti Mahal (Pearl Mosque). The fort is open every day of the week. The entry fee is 50 paisa (free on Fridays).

Chandni Chowk — literally meaning 'moonlight square' — is a vibrant, throbbing, shriekingly loud and colourful shopping area amidst narrow cobbled lanes. It also houses a row of jewellers' shops that will sell you jewellery so exquisite as to remind you of the best shops in London, Paris and Rome (understandable, since India exports jewellery to all these places).

▲▲▲Connaught Place/ Janpath — the shopping and business centre. Adjoining Connaught Place (better known as 'C.P.') is Janpath, where the Tourist Office and Central Cottage Industries Emporium are located. The Tourist Office will give you whatever information you need about the entire country. The officers can help you with your itinerary as well as tell you about excursions and package tours.

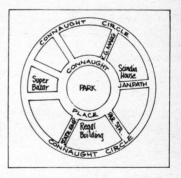

Accommodation

Delhi offers accommodation for all budgets. Its five-star hotels, the **Ashok, Hyatt Regency, Taj Palace, Maurya Sheraton** and **Taj Mahal,** are comparable to the best in the world. The tariffs are also comparable. The ITDC operates some moderately priced hotels, including the **Lodhi, Janpath, Ranjit** and the centrally located **Ashok Yatri Niwas.** Reservations for any of these hotels can be made at the airport.

For budget accommodation, the **YMCA Tourist Guest House** in Parliament Street (Rs 120 (£5) single, RS 200 (£8) double, tel 311561), **Airlines Hotel,** New Delhi Railway Station (Rs 90 (£3.50) single, Rs 135 (£5.50) double) and **Palace Heights,** D

Block Connaught Place (Rs 62 (£2.50) single, Rs 124 (£5) double,
tel. 351369) are good choices. The **International Youth Centre,**
Circular Road, Chanakyapuri (Rs 129 (£5) single and double, Rs
21.50 (£0.85) dormitory, tel. 3013631) is also a good bet. If
you're a Youth Hostel Association member, the **Youth Hostel** on
Nyaya Marg (tel. 3016285) may be your best bet: rooms are only
Rs 19.50 (£0.75) for members, Rs 40.50 (£1.60) for non-members;
it also has a dormitory.

The **Tourist Camping Park** in Jawaharlal Nehru Marg (tel.
278929) is one of the cheaper places to stay in Delhi. In rented
tents the rates are Rs 24-32 (£1-£1.30) single, Rs 36-48 (£1.40-£2)
double, Rs 15 (£0.60) dormitory. If you bring your own tent, the
rates are Rs 10 (£0.40) single, Rs 15 (£0.60) double. The
restaurant offers good food, and you can use the left luggage
room for up to four months at a very nominal charge.

The **Aurobindo Ashram** on Aurobindo Marg (tel. 669225),
about 30 minutes away from Connaught Place, has a lovely
setting and rooms for Rs 50 (£2). They give preference to tourists
with an interest in Indian culture, though how they work that out
remains an abiding mystery.

For convenience, though, it's probably better to choose a hotel
close to Connaught Place and Janpath. **Ringo's Guest House,**
17 Scindia House, Janpath (tel. 3310605) has single rooms for Rs
40 (£1.60) and doubles for Rs 75 (£3). **Sunny Guest House,** 152
Scindia House, Janpath (tel. 3312909) is under the same
management but also has dormitory facilities at Rs 25 (£1). **Asian
Guest House,** 14 Scindia House (tel 3313393 or 3314658) has
rooms from Rs 80 (£3.20) upwards. The **Royal Guest House**
above Sona Rupa restaurant in Janpath (tel. 353485) has single
rooms for Rs 66 (£2.60), double for Rs 80 (£3.20). **Mrs.
Colaco's Guest House,** 3 Janpath Lane (tel. 312558) is
efficiently run and has four rooms and a dormitory with four beds
(Rs 50 (£2) single, Rs 70 (£2.80) double, Rs 25 (£1) dormitory).
Jain Guest House, off Janpath Lane, has five rooms with two
common baths, managed by a physically handicapped advocate
and his family (Rs 50 (£2) single, Rs 70 (£2.80) double).

The Bengali Market area, 20 minutes' walk from Janpath, has a
number of guest houses in the same price range. The better
known ones are **Roshan Guest House, Skylark** and **Blue
Bright.**

The Paharganj area, close to the New Delhi Railway Station,
has many cheap lodgings. Often young tourists head for them and
come away quite satisfied, but many others have bitter
experiences. A number of gentlemen you're likely to meet here
are anxiously sought by Interpol. Drug peddling is rife, and it's a
kind of mini-United Nations of hashish. It can be quite an
adventure.

Food

Nowhere is the Indian zest for food more in evidence than in
Delhi. Though Chinese and Continental food are available and
popular, the city specialises in Mughlai and *tandoori* food,
brought to Delhi by the Mughals and the warlike Pathan tribes
from the northwest. The Pathan carried the *tandoor* (a clay oven)
with them on their travels and lit it wherever they camped.
Tandoori fare usually includes hot, crisp whole wheat tandoori
rotis (bread) and roasted *kababs* and *tikkas* of mutton or chicken.
With timebound rituals of hand pounding, grinding, marinating
and cooking over special fires, the cuisine is prepared carefully
from traditional recipes.

Mughlai food is especially good in the walled city, Old Delhi.
The fare is mainly non-vegetarian. Try **Karim's** (Jama Masjid,
tel 262080), one of the most popular places for connoisseurs of
Mughlai food. They also have a branch in Nizammuddin in
South Delhi. **Moti Mahal** (Daryaganj, tel 273011) specialises in
delicious tandoori chicken preparations. **Jawahar** (Jama Masjid,
tel. 270839) has very reasonably priced Mughlai fare. **Flora**
(Urdu Bazaar, Jama Masjid, tel. 264593) is famous for its heavily
spiced dishes with rich gravy. A decent meal in any of the above
places costs about Rs 50 (£2) a head.

New Delhi also has various barbecues offering traditional
Mughlai and tandoori food. In South Delhi, **Moet's** in Defence
Colony Market (tel. 626814) is very popular, with both a
restaurant and a take-away. It opens at 18:30 every evening.
Chic-Fish in Malviya Nagar, South Delhi, is a smaller street-
corner eatery where the barbecue is excellent and you can have a
Mughlai meal for less than Rs 40 (£1.60). It is closed on
Tuesdays and open on other days only after 18:00.

Two points: first, it's best to select kababs that are not made of
minced meat. (You never know exactly what has been minced.)
And second, Indian food is meant to be eaten with your fingers.
It's practically impossible to handle it with knives and forks, so
don't be embarrassed to use your hands. Ignore the chortling
locals.

Delhi also offers the myriad regional specialities of India, of
which Kashmir and South Indian cuisine are unique. A must are
the famous South Indian *dosas*. Recommended places for South
Indian food (vegetarian) are **Woodlands** in the Lodhi Hotel (tel.
619422) and **Dasaprakash** at the Hotel Ambassador (tel.
690391), both in South Delhi.

Dhahas are open-air roadside restaurants with makeshift wooden
chairs and tables. The food is highly spiced but the atmosphere
convivial and informal. Intended for the poorer people, they can
be dimly discerned behind their veils of dust, flies and fumes. It's
better to admire them at a distance as testimony to the

indestructibility of Indians.

Chinese and Continental food are available in all areas. In the Connaught Place area are **Bercos** in E Block and **Nirula's Chinese Room** in L Block. For Continental food try **Gaylord** or **The Cellar**, both in the Regal Building. In South Delhi, **Chungwa** and **Akasaka** in Defence Colony and **Daichi** in South Extension serve good food at reasonable prices.

Alcohol is available in various wine shops. The 1st and 7th of each month are 'dry days'. Those dates are paydays, and the government believes the population will race to the wine shops to blow their salary. All big hotels and some restaurants have bars licensed to serve alcohol. Indian beer is particularly recommended. You can get whisky, gin, vodka and various wines at 'English wine shops'. Local brews, available everywhere, are cheaper, potent, but best avoided. You can never be sure whether they are adulterated with harmful substances.

Helpful Hints

For medical assistance, go to the All-India Institute of Medical Sciences in South Delhi (tel. 661123) or the Freemasons Polyclinic on Tolstoy Marg (very close to Connaught Place; tel. 312929). The chemist at the government-owned Super Bazaar in Connaught Place is open round the clock (tel. 3310163).

Delhi is, statistically speaking, one of the safest major cities in the non-Communist world. It's a very large city, however, with all sorts of residents. It is best, particularly for women, not to go out unescorted after dark.

TOUR 2

DELHI

If you decide to take the guided tour offered by Delhi Tourism,
you'll see the Jantar Mantar, Laxmi Narayan Temple, Baha'i
Temple, the Qutab Minar and (for some utterly incomprehensible
reason) the Jawaharlal Nehru Stadium. The tariff, inclusive of
entry and guide fee, is Rs 14. Ashok tours are slightly more
expensive. If you decide instead to wander on your own, here is a
plan for seeing Delhi's 'must-sees'.

Suggested Schedule

08:00	Leave for Qutab Minar.
10:00	Humayun's Tomb.
11:00	Purana Quila.
12:00	Jantar Mantar.
13:30	Lunch at Connaught Place.
14:30	Museum.
16:30	Shanti Vana, Rajghat.
19:30	Son-et-Lumiere show at the Red Fort.

Sightseeing Highlights

▲▲▲**Qutab Minar** — The Qutab Minar is a commemorative
tower built by Allauddin Khilji in the 13th century. It is five
storeys high, each storey clearly distinguished by a projecting
balcony. The buildings around are also worth wandering through.
In Sri Aurobindo Marg in South Delhi, the Qutab Minar is
rather badly connected by buses from Connaught Place. A scooter
from C.P. will cost between Rs 18 and Rs 20.

▲▲▲**Humayun's Tomb** — on Mathura Road near the Old
Fort (Purana Quila) — was built in the mid 16th century by Haji
Begum, wife of the second Mughal Emperor, Humayun. It
displays characteristics of the Mughal style with high arches and
double domes, and is considered the forerunner of the Taj Mahal.
On Fridays there is no entrance fee, otherwise it's 50 paise.

▲▲▲**Purana Quila (The Old Fort)** — about 3 km from
Connaught Place — rises on a small hill and is broken at many
points. It overlooks the zoo. The fort is believed to have been
built by Sher Shah, the Afghan ruler who wrested the throne of
Delhi from Humayun, briefly interrupting the power of the
Mughal empire. According to many, the city of Indraprastha

mentioned in the epic *Mahabharatha* was situated here. There is no entrance fee. The adjacent museum is worth a visit. It houses valuable finds from the fort.

▲▲▲**Jantar Mantar** — This observatory, set amidst a garden of stately palms a short walk from Connaught Place, was built by Raja Jai Singh of Jaipur. (The observatory at Jaipur is more impressive.) The Samrat Yantra or Supreme Instrument, the largest piece, is actually a sundial. The other five pieces indicate the movement of the sun, moon and other celestial bodies.

▲▲▲**Rajghat** and **Shantivana** are both located on the Ring Road, about 4 km from the Red Fort. Memorials to Mahatma Gandhi and Jawaharlal Nehru, they exude an atmosphere of peace and tranquillity.

▲▲▲**The National Museum** — south of Rajpath, about 1 km from Janpath — gives a good idea of India's heritage. A fascinating collection of artifacts spans hundreds of years. The Museum has a beautiful collection of Indian bronzes, terracottas and wood sculptures dating back to the Mauryan period. It also has a vast collection of miniature and mural paintings. There are regular film shows highlighting specific periods.

The **National Gallery of Modern Art** near India Gate is another must. It chronicles and encapsulates the development of modern Indian art.

▲▲▲**Son-et-Lumiere** — This is what you see in the evening at the Red Fort. The sound and light show very effectively captures the history of India. The show in English is from 19:30 to 20:30. Entrance tickets are Rs 4 and Rs 8. The open-air show is held throughout the year except during the monsoons.

Vayudoot Himalayan Air Trek

A very unusual experience is the Vayudoot Himalayan Air Trek, which operates throughout the year except during the monsoons, offering an overview of the Garhwal and Kumaon Himalayas. The flight travels at low altitude over Dehradun, Rishikesh, Rudraprayag, Kanol and Kedarnath, the revered pilgrim centre in the Himalayas, to afford a magnificent view of the river Ganga coming down the mountains and its confluence with other rivers en route. Contact: Vayudoot Airlines, tel. 699272, 3312587 or 3312779.

TOUR 3

JAIPUR

From one capital to another — this time Jaipur, the capital of the desert state of Rajasthan. Rajasthan means 'abode of kings', and it truly exudes a regal grandeur. Magnificently ornate palaces and impressive fortresses contrast with the stark desertscape. The Rajputh were a martial race and their folklore, arts, crafts, theatre and dance reflect themes of courage and valour. The people, among whom were my ancestors, had more brawn than brains. They regularly got into wars they lost. When they didn't have outsiders to fight, they fought each other. Not surprisingly, the state is full of forts and weapons. My theory about the endless wars is that the weather is so hot and awful, fighting was a relief.

Suggested Schedule

06:40	Departure from Delhi.
07:15	Arrival Sanganer Airport.
08:30	Check into hotel. Book ticket to Agra for tomorrow morning.
09:30	City sightseeing.
14:00	Visit the Amber Palace & Fort, 11 km away.
Evening	Free for shopping, wandering around the city and its exotic bazaars. If a folk cultural programme is on, don't miss it. Round off the day with a typical Rajasthani vegetarian meal.

Jaipur

Jaipur is Rajasthan's largest city, with a population of over 900,000. Known as the 'Pink City of India', Jaipur is dotted with pink sandstone buildings that add colour and reflect an old world charm. Jaipur derives its name from an astronomer prince, Sawai Jai Singh II, who built the city in 1727. Cradled by the rocky Aravalli hills, the city is divided into seven rectangular blocks built on the basis of the ancient Hindu treatise on architecture, the *Shilpa Shastra*. Reinforcing its martial image is a huge fortified wall that encircles the old city. Jaipur seems chiselled out of the desert. Exquisite buildings in pink terracotta, with delicate filigree work on overhanging porticos and balconies, are echoes of a bygone age.

At an altitude of 431 metres above sea level in the Thar Desert, Jaipur boils during the summer months with temperatures going up to 41 degrees C. The best time to visit Jaipur is in the relatively cooler months between October and March. The northeast part of Jaipur is the old, walled, pink city. The new city spreads itself south and west of the old one.

Mirza Ismail Road (M.I. Road) is the main road in the new Jaipur. Most commercial establishments, modern restaurants and government emporia are situated along this road. The Rajasthan Tourism Office is within the railway station complex. This complex like all railway stations in India, exists in the state of 'functioning anarchy' which, former U.S. Ambassador John Kenneth Galbraith said, characterises India. It's crowded and chaotic, but it works. The Indian Airline city office is on Sanjay Marg in the newer part of the city.

A familiar sight in Jaipur streets are the slow-moving carts drawn by haughty camels sedately chewing their cud as they give the human race withering looks. Visit Bapu Bazaar or Nehru Bazaar. Soak in the colours, the sounds, the camels! It is fascinating. As for shopping, the precious and semi-precious stones of Jaipur are famous as are its textiles and costume jewellery.

Languages commonly spoken are Hindi, Rajasthani and English.

Transport

Jaipur's Sanganer airport, 16 km from the city, is an ancient, homely structure. Auto rickshaws and taxis are available to the city. The one-way fare for auto rickshaws is Rs 25 (£1) and for taxis Rs 45 (£1.80). Both auto rickshaws and taxis are unmetered and fares are negotiable — which means you're in for a fierce haggle. Your chances of beating down the pirates depend on the number of other tourists who've disembarked with you: the more there are, the higher the price. It's best to try and team up with a few other people and share the taxi price. Auto rickshaws are only meant to carry two passengers and taxis five, though like most driving regulations in India, these are cordially ignored.

Auto rickshaws and cycle rickshaws are the popular means of transport in Jaipur. The city bus service is also quite regular but far too crowded. Cycle rickshaws with their toiling, sweating, skinny pedallers, seems a particularly inhumane way to travel, and you may feel foolishly like Simon Legree (or the Brown Man's Burden) but it's quite acceptable. However, settle the fare before hiring one. A cycle rickshaw from the Gangaur Tourist Bungalow to the Hawa Mahal (a 20 minute ride) will be about five rupees. Auto rickshaws charge slightly more. Taxis cannot be hailed on the streets and are generally hired for Rs 200 (£8) for the day. Your hotel manager can advise you.

A half-day sightseeing trip organised by the Tourist Department

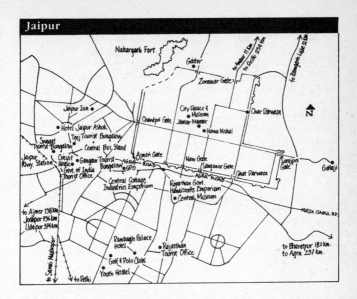

costs Rs 20 (£0.80). However, Jaipur has many attractive sights
and it may be a good idea to sightsee at your own pace. It is
likely to be more rewarding than a conducted tour. You can hire
a guide for half a day from the Transport Department at the
Gangaur Tourist Bungalow at a fixed rate of Rs 30 (£1.20). From
Hawa Mahal to Amber Fort, a round trip in an auto rickshaw
costs Rs 20 (£0.80) (waiting time included). The City Palace, the
Observatory and the Hawa Mahal are within walking distance
from each other. The old city's roads are winding, jam-packed,
colourful, noisy, smelly, quite wonderful. Wander through them.

Hawa Mahal, the Observatory and the City Palace Museum are
in the old city, and so is Johari Bazar, literally meaning the
jewellers' market. In Jaipur you can pick up precious and
semiprecious stones as well as the traditional *meenakari*
(enamelled) jewellery. Traditional crafts make good gifts to take
home. Rajasthan fabric comes in beautiful colours, either block-
printed or tie-and-dyed.

Sightseeing Highlights
▲▲▲**Hawa Mahal (The Palace of Winds)** — The landmark
of Jaipur is the Hawa Mahal, a pale pink sandstone building with
honeycomb designs which derives its name from the cool westerly
winds that blow through it. Five storeys high, it has small
windows each with its own balcony. Built by Maharaja Sawai
Pratap Singh in 1799 AD, it has a spectacular pyramidal façade.

The guide will show you the exterior asking you to 'make a picture'. But do make an effort to see its interior. The entrance is from the rear, and as you climb you will get an excellent view of the city. From the overhanging windows with their latticed screens, the ladies of the court who were in *purdah* (that is, they could not be seen by men) would watch life in the city below. The Hawa Mahal is part of the City Palace complex. Entry fee: Rs .50. Open 10:00 to 17:00 hours.

▲▲▲**City Palace and Museum** — To the west of the Hawa Mahal, in the midst of the fortified old city, lies the City Palace, an imposing blend of traditional Rajasthani and Mughal architecture. The royal family of Jaipur still uses a part of it. Gayatri Devi, the Maharani, who was once included in *Vogue's* list of the world's ten most beautiful women, turned her interest towards active politics. Her son, popularly known as 'Bubbles', is a world famous polo player. Within the city palace are a number of halls, with a splendid marble paved gallery, the fairly modern-looking Mubarak Mahal built by the Maharaja in 1900 and the seven-storey Chandra Mahal. The museum has a rich collection of royal apparel, carpets, an armoury of old weapons, miniature paintings depicting different themes and various other interesting items. The huge three-dimensional painting of Maharaja Jai Singh has a disconcerting way of looking at you wherever you stand. Entry fee: Rs 6. Open 0930 to 1645 hrs.

▲▲▲**Jantar Mantar (The Observatory)** — As old as the city of Jaipur is this famous observatory just across the City Palace. Built in 1726 AD by Sawai Jai Singh, the astronomer king, this is the biggest of all the five observatories he built in India, the Jantar Mantar in Delhi being another of them. Each construction in this observatory has specific purposes such as measuring the exact position of stars or calculating eclipses. The sundial accurately tells you the time of day. I suggest you use a guide here, to reveal the workings of the curious structures to you. Entry fee: Rs 1. Open 09:00 to 17:00 hrs.

Govind Devji Temple — Within the City Palace complex is the temple of Lord Krishna. Krishna, an incarnation of Vishnu, is one of the most endearing deities of the Hindu pantheon, though 'endearing' is probably not the term that has come to your mind when you've run into his saffron-robed Hare Krishna devotees singing to you for alms at airports and elsewhere in Britain and Europe.

▲▲▲**Central Museum** — Also known as Albert Hall, the museum lies south of the walled city in the sprawling Ram Niwas Garden. The Durbar Hall, built in 1887 AD, has a pleasant blend of oriental and Victorian architecture. The museum has an impressive collection of metalware, ivory carvings, jewellery, textiles, pottery, sculptures and paintings and presents an

interesting depiction of Rajasthani rural life. Entry fee: Rs 1.
Open 10:00 to 17:00 hours.

▲▲▲**Amber Palace and Fort** — Eleven km away from the
city and perched amidst rocky hills, Amber (pronounced 'Aamer')
was the ancient capital of Jaipur state. Construction of this
fortress palace was started in 1592 by Raja Man Singh, the
Rajput commander of the Mughal Emperor Akbar's army. The
fort has a majestic presence with its terraces and ramparts
overlooking Maota Lake below.

Within the palace is the Jai Mandir, or Hall of Glory, with its
justly famed Sheesh Mahal, the glittering Hall of Mirrors, its
walls exquisitely inlaid with thousands of tiny mirrors. For a
small tip the attendant will light a match and suddenly the room
is irridescent with light as the match reflects from the walls.
Opposite the Jai Mandir is the Sukh Niwas, or Hall of Pleasures,
with beautiful inlay work.

Another highlight of visiting Amber is the ever-popular
elephant ride up the hill. A bedecked elephant carrying three or
four people costs Rs 60 (£2.40) for a ride. If you decide to walk
up, it will take you 10 to 15 minutes.

A regular bus service connects Amber Palace with the Hawa
Mahal every half hour. One-way tariff is Rs 1.20. You can get an
auto rickshaw — a one-way trip from the Hawa Mahal costs Rs
10. You can share the auto with someone else and reduce the
costs to Rs 5. Entry fee: Rs 1. Timings: 09:00 to 16:30 hrs.

There are some other interesting places around Jaipur like the
cenotaphs at **Gaitor,** towards the north of the city. These were
built in memory of the former rulers. These are gracefully
pillared **chattris** of white marble decorated with fine carvings.
Those of the queens are some distance away. The cenotaph of
Sawai Jai Singh II is one of the most beautiful. **Sisodi Palace
and Garden** (8 km) and **Sanganer Village** (16 km) are worth
visiting. Sanganer is famous for its hand block printed fabrics and
yard lengths drying in the sun present a colourful picture.

Accommodation
There are three government-owned Tourist Bungalows, all near
each other: the **Gangaur Tourist Bungalow** (Tel. 60231 to 38),
the **Teej Tourist Bungalow** (tel. 65538) and the **Swagatam
Tourist Bungalow** (Tel. 67560). Tariffs are Rs 40 (£1.60)
upwards for a single room. Taj has a dormitory at Rs 12 per bed.
All the government Tourist Bungalows are neat and comfortable,
with all the basic facilities. Gangaur has a 24-hour coffee shop
called Gauri.

The **Tourist Hotel** (tel. 64133-35) on M.I. Road, is large and
spacious, with about 50 good sized rooms (single Rs 20 (£0.80)

and double Rs 30 (£1.20) with attached baths. The management
is good and the location very central.

Hotel Rajmahal (Tel. 61257) on Sardar Patel Marg, off M.I.
Road, has reasonably good rooms with attached baths from Rs 40
(£1.60) upwards. At the same tariff, you can rent a room at **Hotel
Savoy** (Tel. 68962) on M.I. Road. Hotels with rates upwards of
Rs 90 (£3.60) are **Hotel Swagat** (Tel. 67712), **Hotel Arya
Niwas** (Tel. 73456) and **Hotel Bissu Palace** (Tel. 74191).

Jaipur also has a fabulous five-star hotel. The **Rambagh
Palace Hotel** (Tel. 75141), a huge converted palace, is possibly
the best hotel in India. In the evening colourful Rajasthani folk
dances are performed here. Entrance is Rs 25 (£1) for non-hotel
guests. The hotel's all-white Polo Bar is attractive and well
stocked. The room rates are upward of Rs 400 (£16).

Other luxury hotels are the huge sandstone **Welcomgroup
Hotel Mansingh** (Tel. 78771), also a former palace, and **Hotel
Clarks Amer** (Tel. 82216).

Food

There's no better place than Jaipur to initiate yourself into pure
vegetarian food. Visit the **Lakshmi Misthan Bhandar** (LMB).
Here the food is purely vegetarian without a hint of onion, garlic
or ginger. (These are roots, which for some inexplicable reason
Indian vegetarians equate with meat.)

Among the popular restaurants on M.I. Road are **Niros
Kwality, Chanakya** (for vegetarian food) and **Handi** (for
barbecue food). Niros serves good seafood, along with Indian and
Continental dishes. However, seafood so far from the sea is not
recommended. A meal at any of the above will cost between Rs
30 (£1.20) and Rs 40 (£1.60).

Near the General Post Office on M.I. Road are a string of
pavitra bhojanalayas — open-air eating places which are neat and
clean. These are totally vegetarian restaurants serving traditional
Rajasthani fare (very spicy and oily) where you can have a full
meal for Rs 10 (£0.40). The **Radha Govind Bhojanalaya** is the
most popular. The service here is fast and personalised. **Gauri**, at
the Gangaur Tourist Bungalow, is also very reasonably priced and
you can get a good meal for Rs 20 (£0.80).

These places are accustomed to tourists and usually solicitous of
their insides. But do ask them not to put too much chilli in the
food. Rajasthani food is justly revered, even in India, for its
spiciness.

TOUR 4

AGRA/FATEHPUR SIKRI

This afternoon you'll visit India's most famous sight, the Taj Mahal. Agra is not only an unparalleled tourist attraction, but also one of the leading centres for the export of handicrafts and leather goods, and a good place for evening bazaar shopping.

Suggested Schedule

Morning	Travel to Agra by road from Jaipur (237 km), stopping to see Fatehpur Sikri.
13:00	Arrive in Agra, check into accommodation.
15:00	Go around Agra Fort, preferably with a guide.
16:30	Visit the Taj Mahal, one of the genuine wonders of the world. Allow plenty of time to soak in the loveliness.
Evening	Visit Kinari Bazaar, the local market with ancient winding lanes. Shops are open late.

Transport

There is no direct flight from Jaipur to Agra, which is why I recommend going by road rather than waste time changing flights.

Buses run frequently from Jaipur to Agra. Deluxe buses — fare Rs 45 (£1.80) — leave at 07:45, 12:00, 15:15 and 23:00 and take five hours. Express buses — fare Rs 32 (£1.30) — leave at 05:30, 06:15, 09:00, 10:30, 11:00, 11:45, 12:30, 13:30, 14:00, 16:30, 22:00 and 22:30 and take 5½ hours.

Inquire at the Tourist Bungalow in Jaipur for taxi service, which costs Rs 2 per km.

Agra

Located in the state of Uttar Pradesh, Agra has a population of about 800,000. The city is spread out on the western bank of the Yamuna River, at 169 metres above sea level and 204 km from Delhi.

The long Mahatma Gandhi Road runs through the centre of the city. In the northwest is the busy Delhi Gate and Hari Parbat area. The U.P. Government Tourist Bungalow (tel. 77035) is located here. The Government of India Tourist Office (tel. 72377)

is very centrally located on the Mall Road, whereas the U.P.
State Government Tourist Office (tel. 75852) is toward the
southern part of the city on Taj Road.

To the south of the Taj Mahal is Fatehabad Road, where most
of the five-star deluxe hotels are located. The budget hotels are
mostly in the Baluganj area, the Saddar area and outside the
southern gate of the Taj Mahal.

Kinari Bazaar and Jauhari Bazaar, famous local markets with
numerous serpentine lanes and a seemingly endless number of
shops are to the north of Agra Fort. Boisterous shopkeepers vie
with each other for attention. The area is crowded and colourful,
reminiscent of a Middle Eastern souk. You can bargain here, as
in most other private shops.

Agra's exquisite marble inlay work is quite justly famous.
Goods available range from large items like table tops to small
trinket boxes. Take a bit of the Taj back with you. In the bazaar
area you can see craftsmen chiselling away at these marvellous
creations. Other crafts include gold and silver *zari* embroidered
work on belt bags and even tea cosies. Agra is also famous for
carpets. Try shopping in the government emporia where you are
sure of both authenticity and correct prices. The Taj Mahal
complex has a U.P. emporium, Gangotri (tel. 66227).

Languages commonly spoken in Agra are Hindi, Urdu and a
Shakespearean English that bears only a remote resemblance to
the language as it is spoken in most of the world.

Transport

Agra is well-connected to major Indian cities by road, rail and air.
Buses from Jaipur and Delhi terminate at the Idgah Bus Station
(tel. 64198) which is quite central. The Cantonment Railway
Station is in the western part of the city, about 6 km from the
Taj Mahal.

In case you choose to fly rather than go by road, Agra Airport
(tel. 62244) is 8 km away from the city, and the Uttar Pradesh
Tourism Department has a well-staffed information counter there.
A regular coach service runs from the airport to the city. The
return service starts from the Indian Airlines office (tel. 73434) at
Hotel Clark's Shiraz (fare Rs 7). The taxi hire charge to the city
is Rs 45 (£1.80). There is no auto rickshaw stand at the airport,
but you can hire an auto for Rs 30 (£1.20).

There are very few yellow-top taxis in Agra, but unmetered
auto rickshaws and fixed-fare tempos are available for city
transport. The opportunities for overcharging are obviously
greater without meters, but it's a small price to pay to see the
Taj.

The most popular mode of transport in Agra is the cycle
rickshaw. The rickshaw pullers, a chattery, friendly lot and nearly

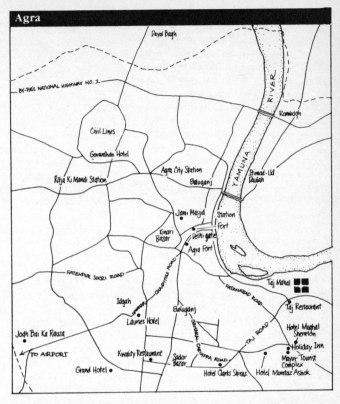

honest, will candidly admit that they are paid a commission for taking tourists to a particular hotel or shop, but at the same time they will not force you into going anywhere in particular. Full day rickshaw fares are about Rs 25 (£1). Rickshaw pullers often insist on being guides as well, but most communicate in English that would make James Joyce giddy with envy — disjointed words, just words, some words neither you nor he have ever heard before, accompanied by grunts, rolling eyes, shrugs and every symptom of an epileptic seizure. Their knowledge of history is flavoured by their own interpretations, what their grandmother once told them, family rumours, the latest theory advanced at their little gatherings, the whole hodge-podge enough to cause any historian to swoon.

Accommodation
Most five-star and deluxe hotels are located in and around

Fatehabad Road about 2 km away from the Taj Mahal. These include the **Welcomgroup Mughal Sheraton** in the deluxe bracket, and **Hotel Mumtaz Ashok**, which has lower rates. The government-owned **Hotel Agra Ashok, Hotel Taj View** (tel. 64171) and **Hotel Clark's Shiraz** (tel. 72421) have rooms at Rs 450 (£18) upwards. **Hotel Amar** (tel. 65696) and the recently opened **Hotel Shahanshah Inn** (tel. 65000), both at Fatehabad Road and centrally air conditioned, provide excellent accommodation at Rs 140 (£5.60) single, 200 (£8) double.

Your best bet is the state-owned **Tourist Bungalow** (tel. 72123) in the Delhi Gate area about 7 km away from the Taj Mahal. It is a neat and comfortable place with singles at Rs 50 (£2), doubles at Rs 75 (£3) and dormitory beds at Rs 15 (£0.60) each. The restaurant at the Tourist Bungalow serves an Indian *thali* for as little at Rs 7. The *thali* is an all-you-can-eat plate comprising several sections, each filled with a small portion of a particular dish. There is also an à la carte menu.

Outside the Tourist Bungalow is the **Ashoka Hotel and Restaurant** (tel. 75108) with singles at Rs 25 (£1) and doubles at Rs 45 (£1.80). Close by is an imposing building, **Hotel Goverdhan** (tel. 66520) with doubles from Rs 40 (£1.60) upwards. The proprietor will introduce himself to you as Dr. Onkar Nath Sharma, M.A., Ph.D., M.A. (USA).

If you wish to be in the centre of the city, the Baluganj area has some good places at reasonable rates. The **Tourist Rest House** (old) is spacious and well maintained. **Hotel Ajay** has rooms from Rs 80 (£3.20) upwards and dormitory beds between Rs 10 (£0.40) and Rs 15 (£0.60). On the same road you'll find another **Tourist Rest House** (new) which has an entirely different management from the one mentioned earlier, and is best avoided.

Major Bakshi's Tourist Home (tel. 76828), centrally located on Ajmer Road, is run by Major Bakshi's widow, a delightful older lady who, with her dedicated staff, looks after the 12 rooms (Rs 80 (£3.20) single, Rs 125 (£5) double). There is no restaurant, but homemade food is served on order. Good place, though overpriced. Major Bakshi's son, Colonel Bakshi, runs another **Bakshi Tourist Home** at Lakshman Nagar on the way to the airport.

The Sadar Bazaar area has a number of hotels and restaurants on the Taj Mahal Road. The one I would recommend is the centrally air-conditioned **Hotel Jaiwal** (tel. 64141 or -2). Their rates start from Rs 125 (£5) single and Rs 175 (£7) double. A 24-hour restaurant serves both vegetarian and non-vegetarian food. A *thali* costs Rs 12.

Near the Agra Fort on General Cariappa Road are two good places to stay. The **Agra Hotel** (tel. 72330), which has been in existence for 62 years, is a huge, sprawling place. The large rooms, each with attached bath, cost Rs 40 (£1.60) single and Rs 60 (£2.40) double. It has camping facilities as well. The restaurant serves Indian, Chinese and Continental food. Excellent value for the money, this place is within walking distance of both the Fort and the Taj. **Hotel Akbar,** also on Cariappa Road, has singles at Rs 35 (£1.40) and doubles at Rs 55 (£2.20). Camping facilities cost Rs 5 per person. This, too, is a good and comfortable place to stay.

Mention must be made of **Hotel Lauries** (tel. 72536) on Mahatma Gandhi Road. In operation since 1865, it is the oldest hotel in Agra, with a charming colonial atmosphere. Part of the hotel building is now let out to commercial establishments, and only 20 rooms remain in the hotel wing (Rs 65 (£2.60) single, Rs 110 (£4.40) double). There are a restaurant, a bar and a swimming pool which is 'being cleaned' most of the time.

The **Mayur Tourist Complex** (tel. 67302) at one end of Fatehabad Road has a beautiful setting with lawns and fountains, and rooms at Rs 90 (£3.60) single, Rs 115 (£4.60) double. The lawns are supposed to be available for camping but are used mostly to host wedding receptions. The youth hostel complex under construction at Sanjay Place should be ready soon (This is India, however, and 'soon' doesn't always mean 'soon soon' but usually 'sometime soon').

If you're looking for really inexpensive accommodation, go to the southern gate of the Taj Mahal complex. In the narrow streets and crooked lanes are a number of lodges and very low-priced hotels, most of them commanding fantastic views of the Taj Mahal from their terrace tops. The three-year-old **Shanti Lodge,** a neat and comfortable place, has 20 rooms from Rs 15 (£0.60) single, Rs 35 (£1.40) double, Rs 6 (£0.24) dormitory. Vegetarian food is served in the main dining hall. The **Shahjahan Hotel and Restaurant,** under the proprietorship of the widely travelled Nisar Ahmed Khan, has been lodging tourists for the last 18 years. The tariff is very reasonable, ranging from Rs 15 (£0.60) to Rs 20 (£0.80). Both vegetarian and non-vegetarian food is served here. The area has a number of other lodges with rock-bottom prices. Since Agra has an acute power crisis, most hotels including many lodges in this area have their own electricity generators.

Food

Most five-star hotels in Agra have restaurants, though the prices are steep. On the Taj Road the **Kwality Restaurant,** and at Hari Parbat the **Capri restaurant,** are air-conditioned and serve excellent food. A proper meal in either of these will be around Rs 40 (£1.60) per person. Kwality also has excellent confectionery.

Recommended at Kwality are any of the chicken curries and Mughlai food. The delicious Chicken Navratan Curry (Rs 22 (£0.90)) was named after the 'nine jewels' (nine ministers) of Emperor Akbar's court — a ninefold palate-pleaser.

The oddly named **Zorba, the Buddha, Rajneesh Restaurant,** not very far from Kwality, is air-cooled, with very pleasant decor. It is run by Dilip Bharti and Anand Bhushan, both disciples of Rajneesh, the controversial Indian guru. Only vegetarian food is served. For an unusual experience, try the Bunny Honey ice cream, deliciously honey-flavoured and served in a glass container shaped like a rabbit. The other dishes have equally exotic names.

If you've sampled south Indian food and have a yen for it, try the **Laxmi Vilas Hotel,** also on Taj Road.

Among other restaurants, ITDC's **Taj Restaurant** serves both Indian and Continental food. **Khaja-Peeja,** near the GPO, used to be good at one time but is now in a shambles.

While in Agra, remember to try Agra's own specialities. Those with a very sweet tooth should try *petha,* a translucent sweet (crystallized marrow), and those with a hot and spicy temperament and taste, *dalmoth* piquant lentils), a crisp, spicy snack. For both, two shops are well-known: **Panchi Petha** in the Delhi Gate area and **Bhimsen Pethawalla** at the fountain in the Sadar area. These are the best, but both *petha* and *dalmoth* are available in various other sweet/snack shops all over the city.

Sightseeing Highlights
▲▲▲**Fatehpur Sikri** — About 37 km west of Agra lies the deserted fortress city of Fatehpur Sikri. Originally it was a small hamlet whose only claim to fame was the presence of the Sufi saint Salim Chishti. As the story goes, Akbar had no male offspring to inherit the great empire he had built. Hearing of the powers of the saint, the great emperor undertook a pilgrimage to invoke his blessings and, miraculously, a son was born to his Hindu wife Jodhabai in 1569. In gratitude, the emperor named his son Salim after the holy saint. Salim later ascended the throne as Emperor Jehangir.

Soon after the birth of his son, Akbar shifted his capital here and, by 1574, most of this palatial city was constructed. Akbar named the city Fatehabad, which was later changed to Fatehpur, meaning 'City of Victory'. For 15 years, from 1570 to 1585, this remained Akbar's capital city and the seat of Mughal power. The guide will tell you that the city was finally abandoned and the capital shifted to Lahore and later back to Agra due to an acute water shortage. But historians claim that Akbar was busy fighting battles, defending and consolidating his empire in the northwest frontier, from 1585 to 1598 during which time he camped at

Lahore. During his absence, Fatehpur was ignored and deteriorated considerably. Later Akbar readopted Agra as his capital and remained there until his death in 1605.

The imperial city of Fatehpur Sikri is rectangular in plan, with nine huge gates on three sides, well protected on the western side by an artificial lake. Assigned to serve as the cultural, commercial and administrative centre of the Mughal empire, it presents an interesting silhouette of shales from a distance. Built entirely of red sandstone, it exhibits a more robust image than the pristine white of the Taj. An interesting blend of styles — Central Asian, Mughal and Hindu Rajput — Fatehpur Sikri is an expression of the emperor's catholicity. Among the monuments worth visiting are **Dewan-i-Am,** the single pillared **Diwan-i-Khas, Jami Masjid, Palace of Jodha Bai, Birbal Bhavan, Panch Mahal** (Wind Tower), **Hawa Mahal** (Wind Palace), **Kabutar Khana** Pigeon House, the **Hiran Minar** (Deer Tower), **Sheikh Salim Chishti's Tomb** and **Khwabgarh** (Akbar's bedroom). You need a minimum of an hour at Fatehpur Sikri — though to do justice to this magnificent city you could well spend more time.

The most impressive structure in Fatehpur Sikri is the **Buland Darwaza** or Victory Gateway, which stands triumphant and forceful. Other than that, you must see the **Jami Masjid,** which also contains the grave of the saint Salim Chishti, surrounded by white filligreed stone walls. Make a wish — if you are sincere and have the willing ear of the saint, they say, it will come true. If it does, you are supposed to come back and offer thanksgiving (making another visit to India a certainty).

The **Sheesh Mahal** is also worth a visit, as is the **Ankh Michauli,** where Akbar played blind man's buff with the ladies of his harem when he wasn't running his empire. The area is decorated with frightening stone monsters.

The diving boys at Fatehpur Sikri are famous in India. For a small fee they will dive from a great height into a deep well below. You will be amazed at their daring, but before you know it they're back happy and smiling, all ready to perform again. Entry: Rs .50.

▲▲▲**Taj Mahal** — 'See the Taj and die,' someone said, and the Taj certainly surpasses description. The builders and architects were careful not to confront the viewer with its dazzling glory all at once. Your first vision of the Taj is through a magnificent arched gateway inscribed with verses from the Koran. Gradually the complete edifice unfolds. The Taj is a monument to love, and every detail has been conceptualized and worked out with care.

According to legend, the Emperor Shahjehan was so grief-sticken at the death of his wife, Mumtaz Mahal, that he decided to erect a memorial to her which would be unsurpassed in beauty and grandeur. He invited designers and architects from far and wide, as the storybooks say. The design finally selected was that of the architect Ustad Isa Khan Effendi from Iran. Construction commenced in 1632. The best marble was transported from Makrana in Rajasthan, and precious stones came from as far away as Afghanistan, Persia and central Asia. With the whole treasury at their command and a huge labour force of 20,000 people, it took 21 long years to complete this masterpiece.

Though there are graves on the first floor, Mumtaz Mahal's actual remains lie below in a subterranean chamber. After her death, the great Emperor wasn't exactly celibate in his grief. He could console himself with some 300 wives and 1000 concubines. According to legend, the people who built the Taj weren't as fortunate. Allegedly the architect was blinded, the artisans had their thumbs cut off and the workers their hands chopped off so they could never again build anything so lovely. It's an unlikely story, but those were bloodthirsty times and various guides swear it's true.

The Taj Mahal stands on a raised marble platform with four tall white minarets, one at each corner. It's actually beyond description and no secondhand information on its perfect craftsmanship and superb marble inlay work can come anywhere near doing it justice. It has to be seen to be believed. Entry Rs 2.

▲▲▲**Agra Fort** — A vast museum of interesting buildings, started by Akbar. Each successive Mughal Emperor right up to Aurangzeb contributed something. Construction of the Agra Fort started in 1565 and was completed in 1573. Spread over a triangular area of one and a half miles, the fort's red sandstone walls are 70 feet high. There are four entrances, the main one being through the exquisitely carved Amar Singh Gate to the south. Akbar built buildings to take care of every necessity, in the same way as he had done at Fatehpur Sikri.

From the Agra Fort one can get a grand view of the Taj Mahal. Shahjehan, the builder of the Taj, was imprisoned in the Agra Fort by his son Aurangzeb. With age and weakening eyesight he could no longer see the Taj clearly and a small mirror was set into the wall to reflect his favourite creation. It is said that he died while gazing at it. Entry: Rs 2.

▲▲▲**Itmad-ud-Daulah's Tomb** — This magnificent marble mausoleum, said to be a forerunner of the Taj, was built by Empress Noorjahan, wife of Emperor Jehangir, in memory of her father Ghiasuddin Beg. Noorjehan's mother is also buried here. There is very fine workmanship and inlay work on the marble arches of this mausoleum. Valuable stones of different colours are carved and set together in beautiful designs, and four minarets give a finished, defined look. A wonderful example of superb Mughal craftsmanship. Entry: Rs 2.

TOUR 5

KHAJURAHO

When I was a boy at school, we were carted once a year around India on what was loftily called an educational tour. We stopped in a dusty little town called Khajuraho, full of some rare temples (a subject somewhat remote from the hearts of small boys).

While some of us clustered round a soft drinks stall, a few of my young friends wandered into the temple complex and soon came racing back. 'Oi oi,' they screamed, 'hurry! There are dirty temples here!'

That, I suppose, is one way of looking at it.

Suggested Schedule	
08:30	Depart from Agra Airport.
09.10	Arrive at Khajuraho Airport.
09:30	Check into hotel.
10:30	Visit the western group of temples.
12:30	Visit the Archaeological Museum, just opposite the western temples.
13:00	Lunch.
14:00	Visit eastern group of temples and Khajuraho village.
16:00	Visit Duladeo Temple, one of the two southern group temples. (The other, Chaturbhuj, is closer to the airport and can be visited on your way to the airport tomorrow.)
17:00	Return to western temples. The evening light is perfect for sculpture photography.
Evening	Hotel Chandela has a cultural programme every evening. The Shiv Sagar Tank near the Western Temples has boating in the evenings when there is enough water.

Khajuraho

Ancient Kharjjuravahaka, the temple city of central India, lies in the state of Madhya Pradesh. It has the distinction of possessing fine, well-preserved temples that represent one of the highest and most prolific movements of the medieval Hindu Renaissance. The erotic carvings on the walls, depicting the act of sex in every conceivable posture (as well as some inconceivable ones), are more than just naughty pictures in stone. They offer a wealth of sublime beauty and superb craftmanship, and the artistic rendering of every detail is nearly outrageous. The most popular theme is woman: reflective, playful, amorous. Other sculptures depict nymphs, beasts, demons in revolt, gods in cosmic evolution, and mortals caught in human emotions such as fear, doubt, jealousy, ardent love and consummate passion.

Today, apart from the temples, there's little else in Khajuraho, a small village that thrives on tourist traffic. Khajuraho is at an elevation of 280 metres above sea level and has a population of less than 5000. The nerve centre is the western group of temples, around which most lodges, restaurants and shops are located. Village Khajuraho and the eastern group of temples are about 1.5 km from there.

The government emporium, Mriganayani, is just across the road from the temples of the western group. There are a number of *thele walas* (cart pushers) selling their wares, mostly figures and toys made of copper. Coin collectors can easily buy 100 to 200 year old Indian coins from these cart pushers. The coins, which are dug out even to this day from areas in and around Khajuraho, sell for Rs 5 to Rs 10 per coin, depending on how dated they are. But do remember that there is a ban on export of antiquities, i.e. items over 100 years old.

The language most commonly spoken in Khajuraho is Bundeli. On the off chance that you don't speak Bundeli, English is also common.

The best time to visit Khajuraho is between October and March. May and June are terribly hot and dusty. The Annual Dance Festival, with a cross-section of dances from all over India, is held in March each year. Many Indian dances evolved in the temples, and to many dancers the festival is a kind of homecoming.

Transport

About 600 km south of Delhi, Khajuraho is connected by both air and road. The nearest railhead, Setna, is about 65 km away.

The Khajuraho Airport (tel. 36) is 5 km away from the centre of town, about a ten-minute drive. Private taxis, available at the airport, charge a fixed fare of Rs 20 to any of the hotels or the temples. There is a Tourist Information counter at the airport (tel. 56; open during flight hours only). Cycle rickshaws also ply between the airport and town (fare Rs 10), but there is no rickshaw stand at the airport. There are no auto rickshaws, either, though a few *tongas* (horse-drawn carriages) can be seen.

The Indian Airlines office (tel. 35) is adjacent to the Hotel

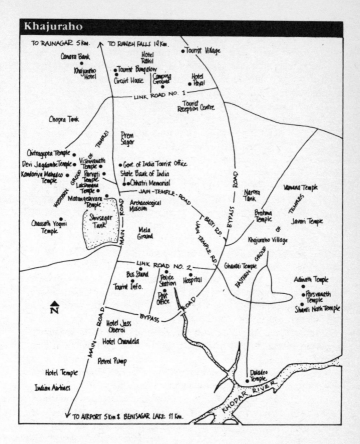

Khajuraho

Temple, about 3 km from the airport on the way to town. The Government of India Tourist office (tel. 47) and the State Bank of India (tel. 29) are opposite the western group of temples. The State Government Tourist Office is opposite the Hotel Khajuraho Ashok.

Taxis cannot be hired off the roads, but private taxis are available from tour operators and the Tourist Office. Fares are Rs 2.20 per km for local excursions. Approved car hire rates are Rs 60 (£2.40) (half-day) and Rs 120 (£4.80) (full day). Cycle rickshaws are readily available, fares are negotiable. Half-day hire for a cycle rickshaw is normally not more than Rs 30 (£1.20). Since distances are short and rickshaws aplenty, it is really not necessary to hire one for the day, only point-to-point.

Khajuraho's bus station, Yashovarman, and the post office (tel. 22) are also quite close to the western temples, behind the cluster of shops and emporia selling souvenirs and an assortment of handicrafts.

Approved guides can be hired through the Tourist Office at Rs 40 (£1.60) for half a day. Many guides operate independently as well. For local assistance of any kind, you can contact an old-time resident, Mr Anant Kumar Khare. He doesn't have a phone, but everyone knows him. To ask for him is to see the bush telegraph in operation.

Sightseeing Highlights

The temples of Khajuraho can be divided into three main geographical groups—western, eastern and southern. A unique feature of the Khajuraho temples is that contrary to the general custom, these temples are not enclosed within a wall but stand on a high terrace of solid elevation above their surroundings. Most of the Khajuraho temples are constructed of granite or sandstone, and the entire mass has a loftiness enhanced by smaller replica turrets grouped around the main tower. The walls are richly adorned with sculptures, pulsating with warmth and vigour.

▲▲▲**The Western Group of Temples**—The largest group in Khajuraho (allow 2 hours to visit them), spread out in beautifully maintained gardens, are the famous Kandariya Temple with its spectacular spire; the Lakshmana Temple, the only one which retains its complete form; the Chitragupta Temple, enshrining the image of the Sun God; the Devi Jagadambe Temple; the Parvati Temple, and the Nandi Temple. All these temples are within a large fenced garden. Entry is Rs 0.50, and the same ticket admits you to the Archaeological Museum as well.

Two of the western temples are outside the garden complex. One is the Matangeshvara Temple, to the south of the Lakshmana Temple. Both its exterior and interior are plain and devoid of sculptured or carved ornamentation. Inside the sanctum is a 2.5 metre high lingam which is worshipped by devotees. The Matangeshvara Temple is considered the holiest of all the Khajuraho temples and is still used for active worship.

The other temple, belonging to the western group but a 10 to 15 minute walk away from the other temples down a dirt track, is the Chausath Yogini Temple, meaning the shrine of the sixty-four female ascetics. This is believed to be the earliest surviving shrine at Khajuraho, made entirely of granite and dedicated to Goddess Kali, whose idol no longer exists.

▲▲▲**Archaeological Museum**—In 1910, loose sculptures and architectural pieces of the ruined temples of Khajuraho were collected and preserved in an enclosure built adjoining the western group of temples. In 1952 it was taken over by the Archaeological Survey of India and classified as a museum. The present museum building, though not large in size, displays a representative collection of the Khajuraho sculptures. A colossal figure of the Dancing Ganesha—a fine piece of sculpture—greets the visitor in the main entrance hall. There are a Jain gallery and a Buddhist gallery as well. The museum is definitely worth a visit; half an hour should be enough.

▲▲▲**Eastern Group of Temples / Khajuraho Village**— About 1.5 km east of the western temples and near the Khajuraho village lies the eastern group of temples. They consist of three Hindu temples—Brahma, Vamana and Javari—and three Jain temples—Ghantai, Adinatha and Parsvanatha. The Adinatha and Parsvanatha are located within a compound, adjacent to each other. You will know you've reached the Jain temples when you see a prominent signboard outside saying 'Smoking and chewing paan strictly prohibited inside.' (*Paan* is a betel leaf.) Parsvanatha is the biggest and finest temple here from the sculptural point of view. Many sculptures reproduced in Khajuraho brochures are from the Parsvanatha Temple. The Adinatha Temple is immediately to the north of the Parsvanatha Temple. In the sculpture of this temple, the artists have been marvellously successful in depicting several emotions in stone. The third Jain temple, Ghantai, is a little away to the south of village Khajuraho. Though in ruins, it still retains evidence of the great artistic skill of its builders. Entry to these temples is free.

The three Hindu temples in the eastern group are scattered in and around the Khajuraho village, quite close to each other in distance. The best way to see them is to go in a cycle rickshaw which can wind its way through the narrow lanes of the village. **Southern Group of Temples** — The group consists of the Duladeo Temple, 2.5 km away, and the Chaturbhuj Temple 4.6 km away from the western group. Standing in isolation, the Duladeo Temple is dedicated to Lord Shiva and, again, has fine sculptures on its main wall. The Chaturbhuj Temple is toward the airport and can be visited en route. It has a huge, exquisitely carved image of Lord Vishnu.

Accommodation

Hotel Chandela (tel. 54) and **Hotel Jass Oberoi** (tel. 66), located next to each other, are five-star luxury hotels. Both have swimming pools which can be used by outsiders on payment of Rs 25 (£1). The central government-owned **Hotel Khajuraho Ashok** (tel. 24) offers singles at Rs 190 (£7.60) and doubles at Rs 250 (£10). The State Tourist Department runs **Hotel Payal** (tel. 76), **Hotel Rahil** (tel. 62) and the **Tourist Village** (tel. 64). Payal has singles at Rs 90 (£3.60) and doubles at Rs 130 (£5.20)—the tariff includes breakfast. Rahil offers singles at Rs 40 (£1.60) and doubles at Rs 60 (£2.40), all with attached baths. Rahil also has a dormitory at Rs 15 (£0.60) per bed. It is a comfortable place with a courteous staff, though a 20-minute walk from the western group of temples. The Tourist Village has singles at Rs 60 (£2.40) doubles at Rs 90 (£3.60), but only a limited number of rooms. The Tourist Village has camping facilities as well.

Opposite the western group of temples, a number of guest houses and hotels offer budget accommodation. **Hotel New Bharat Lodge** (tel. 82) has singles at Rs 40 (£1.60) and doubles at Rs 60 (£2.40), all with attached baths. Dormitory charges are at about Rs 15 (£0.60). The **Jain Lodge** (tel. 52), in operation for the last 21 years, can be safely recommended. It is opposite New Bharat Lodge and has singles at Rs 25 (£1.00) (with common bath) or Rs 35 (£1.40) (with attached bath). Doubles are Rs 30 (£1.20) to Rs 60 (£2.40). The staff here is very hospitable and courteous, and the service is efficient. Excellent value for the money.

There are a number of other budget hotels — **Yadav Lodge Sunset View** (tel. 77), **Hotel Temple** (tel. 49), **Madras Coffee House Hotel** (tel. 44), **Gupta Lodge,** etc. The newly opened **Sheetal Hotel** next to Yadav Lodge has singles with attached baths at only Rs 20 (£0.80).

Food
The coffee shop at **Hotel Chandela,** with its distinctly French ambience, is a good place for a quick bite. A proper meal in either the Chandela or the **Oberoi** will be about Rs 70 (£2.80). Food is excellent at both places.

Just across the western group of temples is a row of *bhojanalayas* where a meal costs about Rs 10. The **Raja Cafe Restaurant,** is run by an Anglo-Indian lady named Joy, who insists the restaurant is under Swiss management since her brother-in-law is Swiss. It's a nice place, spread under shady trees, with an elaborate menu of Indian, Continental and Chinese food. Raja Cafe is a very popular meeting place for tourists. A meal here costs Rs 30 (£1.20) upwards. The management also runs an 'Indian-Swiss Jungle River Village Resort' about 30 km away from Khajuraho.

Close to Raja Cafe is **New Bharat Restaurant,** again an open-air place. Food is reasonable and slightly cheaper than at the Raja. The **Madras Coffee House** is near the Museum. Food is cheap, but surroundings shabby. The **Safari Restaurant,** close to New Bharat, is also all right.

Mineral water sells for Rs 15 per bottle, and beer for Rs 22. Incidentally, the beer everywhere in India is very good, though potent. The alcohol content ranges from 9% to 12%. Generally, the higher the price the greater the alcohol content.

TOURS 6,7 & 8

VARANASI

The oldest continuously inhabited city in the world, contemporary with Babylon, Nineveh and Thebes and already an old city when Rome was founded, Varanasi has been the religious capital of Hinduism almost since its inception. Written records as contained in the *Mahabharatha* and other epics mention its existence at least 3,000 years ago. The Chinese traveller Hiuen Tsang, who visited the city in the 7th century AD, described it as 'a city of great wealth and religious importance'.

Suggested Schedule

Tour 6

09:40	Depart from Khajuraho airport.
10:20	Arrive at airport.
11:00	Reach city, check into hotel, lunch.
15:00	Visit Godaulia, the city's nerve centre. The *ghats* (stone steps down to the river) of Varanasi are an easy walk from here. Wander the numerous streets around Godaulia for a feel of the city.
Evening	Try to see a music/dance programme.

Tour 7

05:30	The U.P. State Road Transport (tel. 43476, 63233) conducts a trip including a boat ride, visits to various temples and the Benares Hindu University.
14:30	Take UPSRT's afternoon guided trip to Sarnath and the Ramnagar Fort.
Evening	Free to visit the *ghats*.

Tour 8

Free day	Go boating, shop, revisit the *ghats,* hire a cycle rickshaw or tonga for a ride through the incredibly congested streets.
17:30	Depart from Varanasi airport.
20:40	Arrive at Calcutta airport, travel to city and check into hotel. If you're not too weary after the flight, go to one of the restaurants in Park Street, which never really goes to sleep.

Varanasi

With a population of about a million, at 80.71 metres above sea level on the west bank of the River Ganga in the State of Uttar Pradesh, Varanasi is about 5 km long from north to south. Languages commonly spoken in Varanasi are Gorakhpuri (close to Hindi), Hindi and English.

From ancient times, Varanasi has been a great religious centre for the Hindus, perhaps the most sacred place of pilgrimage and certainly the most popular as you will immediately discover. Unending streams of pilgrims pour into the city to bathe in the sacred waters of the Ganga. To a pious Hindu, dying in Varanasi is deliverance, the merging of the soul with the Absolute.

For Buddhists, too, Varanasi is a significant destination, for it was at Sarnath, 10 km away, that Lord Buddha preached his first sermon more than 2,500 years ago.

The city has an old and rich cultural heritage—music, dancing and craftsmanship have drawn artists over the ages. Tourists are irresistibly drawn to this mingling, chaotic, colourful city typifying all that is India.

Many Indian cities are renowned for their temples, but only Varanasi has the distinction of having so many *ghats*—about a hundred in all. The city appears from a distance as a series of spires and buildings in gradual descent, almost surrendering themselves to the river. The *ghats* are steps leading to the river, built by kings, businessmen, and philanthropists after whom they have been named. The burning *ghats* might be a rather repellant sight, unless you appreciate their spirit. For Hindus, being cremated at Varanasi is the ultimate blessing, so you'll find bodies lined up waiting to be burned. The *ghats* of Varanasi hum with activity night and day. Chanting starts early in the morning, before sunrise. Thousands of people, both pilgrims and residents of the city, come to bathe, many performing the ritual of *surya namaskar* or sun worship. The rapt, intent expressions speak of the unshakeable faith of the people who can be seen bathing, worshipping and meditating.

Close to the riverfront are the popular areas of Chowk, Lahurabir and Godaulia. The city centre is around the Godaulia and Lohurabir areas, where most budget hotels and restaurants are located. The Cantonment area, a little way away, forms the new part of the city with its wide, well-planned roads.

Varanasi is also a shopper's paradise. (I hate to keep calling places 'shoppers' paradises', but, as you'll often hear in India, 'What to do?') I say this not just in terms of the staggering variety the city offers, but also the atmosphere of the shopping centres. The lane leading to the Vishwanath Temple contains all that Varanasi has to offer, complete with colour, noise, confusion and cows. You'll find the shopkeepers calling out in English,

French, Italian or German depending on where they think the tourists are from. It's amazing how they can tell instinctively, instantly—and usually wrongly.

Shop in Varanasi for its fabulous brocade in yard lengths or in the form of stoles. Other typically Varanasi crafts are stoneware, brass, and carpets which are hand knotted and come in both the Aubusson and Persian variety. Shop at the government emporia in Nadesar where the price is fixed and the quality assured. If, however, you feel confident enough to handle Varanasi on your own, you can try other shopping areas including Chowk and Godaulia. Bargaining is a must. Prices are inflated to almost double the value. Happy haggling.

Transport

Varanasi is well connected by air, rail and road with other major cities of India. The airport, Babatpur (tel. 42832) is 22 km from the city. An Airlines Coach Service operates at certain fixed times. The fare to the city airline office is Rs 20. (£0.80). Private taxis from the airport to the city charge a fixed fare of Rs 95 (£3.80). Auto rickshaws do not operate between the airport and the city. The Indian Airlines city office is at Mint House Motel (tel. 43116, 43146) in the Cantonment area. Cycle rickshaws from the airline office to Godaulia will cost about Rs 10. There is a Tourist Information counter at the airport, open only during flight hours.

There are no taxis available off the roads, though private taxis can be hired. Approved taxi operators include UPSTDC (tel. 43486), Benares Tours (tel. 42401) and the exotically named De Paris Transport Service (tel. 42464), which has nothing to do with Paris. In addition, various tour operators and hotels can arrange for taxi hire. Taxi charges for a full day (90 km or 8 hours) are Rs 225 (£9.00), with an extra Rs 2.50 per kilometre. Tempo rickshaws, available for point-to-point travel, take six to eight people. Minimum fare is Rs 2. Auto rickshaws, though not many, are also available—minimum fare Rs 2.50.

Cycle rickshaws are the most popular form of conveyance. Varanasi has a total of about 40,000 licensed cycle rickshaws and it often looks as though the city has been taken over by them. The rickshaws are the cheapest and most comfortable way of moving around in the chaotic traffic of the city. The rickshaw driver warns other road users of his presence by violently ringing a piercingly loud little bell and by viciously cursing anyone who comes in his path. Since inevitably many do, thoroughfares sound as though armies of homicidal maniacs are rampaging through them. However, physical battles never seem to occur.

Another interesting way to observe the city is to take a boat trip. An hour-long journey costs about ten rupees, less if you

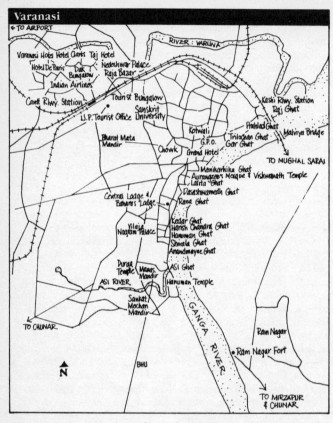

share the boat with others. Since dead bodies are immersed in the
Ganga, it's not a terribly good idea to let your hand dangle idly
in the waters while drifting dreamily down. You may meet an old
friend (or parts of him).

Sightseeing Highlights
All the sights mentioned below are included in guided sightseeing
trips offered by Uttar Pradesh State Road Transport (tel. 43476,
63233), starting from the Tourist Bungalow, Parade Kothi, with
pick-up points on the way.
▲▲▲**The Ghats**—Varanasi and its ghats are synonymous. It's
the ghats which lend the city its unique character. Godaulia leads
to the main ghat, Dasaswamedh, which is vibrant with a religious
atmosphere at all times. This is also the terminal for boat trips,
and a cluster of boats are moored here. Cane umbrellas shade
priests and holy men who perform religious ceremonies for

pilgrims arriving here. And of course the bathers are there taking a holy dip in the sacred river. In the very early hours of the morning this particular ghat is a fascinating place.

The best way to see all the ghats is by taking a boat trip. Each ghat unfolds its unique sights as the boat goes past the curve of the river. The Harishchandra and the Manikarnika are the two burning ghats used for cremations. At Manikarnika, cremations go on round the clock. Photography at both burning ghats is very strictly prohibited.

Some other ghats you sail past are the Kedar Ghat, Hanuman Ghat, Tulsidas Ghat, Mir Ghat, Lalita Ghat and Gai Ghat, each with its own myths and legends.

▲▲▲**Vishwanath Golden Temple**—Close to Dasaswamedha is the most sacred temple of Varanasi, the Vishwanath, dedicated to Lord Shiva, the patron deity of the city. Known as the Golden Temple because of its plated dome, it stands next to a mosque which was built by the Mughal Emperor Aurangzeb after destroying the original temple. The present Golden Temple was built in the year 1776. An unending stream of pilgrims visits this popular temple. Non-Hindus are not allowed entry into the temple, but from the terrace top of the Trimurti Guest House close by you can get a magnificent view of the golden spire.

▲▲▲**Durga Temple**—Goddess Durga is a manifestation of Parvati, the consort of Lord Shiva, and this 18th century temple is dedicated to her. It's also known popularly as the Monkey Temple because hordes of monkeys inhabit it. An interesting place for taking photographs, but be careful—the monkeys can be aggressive. There is a corridor on the first floor from which you can look into the temple, as entry is prohibited to non-Hindus. This is a regrettable feature of Varanasi, but the city is so suffused with tradition that beliefs outmoded two thousand years ago still prevail.

▲▲▲**Tulsi Manas Temple**—Adjacent to the Durga Temple, this temple was built in 1964 by a philanthropist family of Varanasi. The entire epic *Ram Charit Manas* is engraved on the white marble covering the walls of the temple. You're in luck: for a charge, non-Hindus are allowed into this temple.

▲**Bharat Mata Temple**—An unusual temple, it has a marble relief map of India dedicated to Mother India, i.e. the nation as mother, instead of any gods or goddesses. A good lesson in geography, nothing much otherwise.

▲▲▲**Sarnath**—10 km away. Here Lord Buddha preached his first sermon. In the 3rd century BC, Emperor Ashoka is said to have built several monuments here including the monolithic pillar (preserved in Sarnath Museum) a part of which is now India's national emblem. Sarnath was once the cradle of Buddhism. The Dhamek Stupa is the most important stupa here. The museum

has a rich collection of art objects. Tempos charge Rs 5 one-way
to Sarnath from Godaulia. Buses are cheaper but crowded.

▲▲▲**Benares Hindu University**—Covering an area of about
2,000 acres, this is perhaps the largest residential university in
Asia and a great seat of Oriental learning. A notable feature of the
campus is the Bharat Kala Bhawan (art gallery) with its large
collection of rare art objects including paintings for which the
gallery is famous. The university campus is beautifully spread out
and lined with lovely trees, totally different from the streets of
the city centre. A rickshaw from Godaulia to BHU will charge Rs
8 to 10 one-way.

▲▲**Ramnagar Fort**—On the other side of the Ganga River the
residential palace of the Maharaja of Varanasi is included in the
conducted tour. Otherwise, take a ferry across from Asi Ghat.
The Royal Museum contains an impressive collection of silver
and brocade palanquins, silver howdahs for elephant riding, and
an armoury.

Accommodation

Most of the five-star hotels in Varanasi are in the Cantonment
area. One of the cheaper hotels there is the state-owned **Tourist
Bugalow** (tel. 43413) at Parade Kothi, a short walk from the
railway station. Singles are Rs 35 (£1.40), doubles Rs 50 (£2.00),
all with attached baths. Dormitory beds are Rs 15 (£0.60) per
bed. Just outside the Tourist Bungalow on the road leading to the
station are a number of low-priced hotels. **Hotel Amar** (tel.
43509) has singles as Rs 35 (£1.40) and doubles at Rs 50 (£2.00)
with attached baths. Rooms with common baths are of course
cheaper. **Hotel Relax** has a similar tariff. The **Mint House
Motel** (tel. 43089), where the airline office is located, is at
Nadesar in the Cantonment area. Singles are Rs 30 (£1.20) and
doubles at Rs 50 (£2.00). The only disadvantage with hotels in
the Cantonment and station areas is that they are at an
inconvenient distance from Chowk, the city centre, so you miss
being in the heart of things. Of course, the advantage is that the
area is less crowded and noisy.

There are a large number of comfortable yet cheap hotels in the
ghats area around Godaulia. **Yogi Lodge** (tel. 53986) in Kalika
Street, run efficiently by Mr. Lance, his son Ronnie and his
glamorous mother Lorna, has been popular with budget tourists
for at least ten years. Every rickshaw puller knows it. In one of
the many streets between Godaulia and Chowk, it can
accommodate about 50 guests at a time. The rooms are tiny but
well-ventilated. One disadvantage is that none of the rooms have
attached baths, but Yogi Lodge makes up for it with a jovial
atmosphere. It has an air-cooled lounge with music and a
restaurant serving simple vegetarian meals. Tariff is Rs 20 (£0.80)

single, Rs 30 (£1.20) double. Dormitories are Rs 10 (£0.40) per bed. Good central place, though a bit closed-in from all sides. The view from the roof is fabulous.

If you're looking for a less congested place, the **Tandon Lodge** (tel. 62528), at Gai Ghat toward the north of the city, is both neat and pretty. Two km from the city airline office and a ten-minute walk from the post office, singles cost Rs 20 (£0.80) and doubles Rs 30 (£1.20) with attached baths. Tandon Lodge overlooks the riverfront, commanding a beautiful view of the ghats. A walk from here to Chowk or Godaulia along the ghats takes a good 30 minutes. Cycle rickshaws take as much time due to the congested traffic. Tandon Lodge is a lovely, quiet place, serving only vegetarian food.

Besides Yogi and Tandon Lodge, a couple of other places can be recommended. The **Garden Lodge** in the heart of the city, opposite the Sushil Cinema in Godaulia, is set amidst gardens with a lot of open space. Singles come for Rs 25 (£1.00) and doubles for Rs 40 (£1.60) with attached baths. The Garden Lodge is excellent value for money. **Hotel K.V.M.** (tel. 63749) near Garden Lodge also has singles at Rs 25 (£1.00) and doubles at Rs 55 (£2.20) with attached baths.

Lohurabir area hotels include **Hotel Ajay** (tel. 43707), **Hotel International** (tel. 67140), **Hotel Natraj** (tel. 43612), **Modern Lodge** (tel. 63213) and many others which offer budget accommodation.

Back toward the ghats in the city centre, another recommended place is the three year old **Trimurti Guest House** at Saraswati Phatak. Singles are Rs 20 (£0.80) and doubles Rs 35 (£1.40), all with attached baths. Its greatest asset is the fantastic view you get of the golden spire of the Vishwantha Temple, just two streets away. The management is courteous and very helpful.

The list of hotels in this city with its heavy tourist inflow is really endless. The ones mentioned here are but a few.

Food
Varanasi has some excellent vegetarian restaurants. The **Tulsi Restaurant,** just six years old but very popular, is near Prakash Cinema in Lohurabir. It serves a wide variety of vegetarian food, with 115 items on the menu. Try the Tulsi Navratan Pulav, a deliciously flavoured red rice dish (Rs 15). Among the desserts, try the Ras Malai Kesar Badaam, which at Rs 7 per plate is quite delectable but perhaps oversweet for western palates. Close to Lohurabir, in the Maldahiya area, the **Nagina Restaurant** (tel. 43650) of Hotel Jai Ganges serves Indian, Chinese and Continental food and has quite a pleasant atmosphere.

In Godaulia, a popular open-air place is the **Aces Health Food Restaurant.** It doesn't look very clean, but tourists claim that the food here never affects their stomachs adversely. This, presumably, is why it's called health food.

Winfa, in a street adjacent to Prakash Cinema in Lahurabir, is a very popular Chinese restaurant. The prices are reasonable and the food is good. Try the Chicken with Cashew Nuts (Rs 18). You get eight pieces of chicken topped with nuts. You can have a decent non-vegetarian meal at Winfa for less than Rs 30 (£1.20).

In the Godaulia area are some cheap *bhojanalayas* where Rs 10 can get you a full meal. The **Akash Ganga Sweets and Cafe** is a decent place where a plate of *puris* (a fluffy bread) and potatoes costs only Rs 3. The **Sardar Restaurant,** also very reasonably priced, is a popular eating place.

If you're feeling rich, the luxury hotels in the Cantonment area have some excellent restaurants, though eating there is like eating in any other big city hotel.

Varanasi's sweets and *paan* (betel leaf and condiments) are famous and both have a range and variety that is staggering. For sweets, the most popular shop is **Kshir Sagar** in Sonarpura with a branch in the Chowk area. A typical Varanasi sweet, which you're likely to spot in other sweet shops as well, is called *tirangi,* which is in the same three colours as India's national flag. Indian sweets are achingly sweet, so it's best to buy one piece at a time and experiment gingerly.

A *paan* is uniquely Indian concoction. It leaves the mouth red. If you see streets full of people all appearing to spit out blood, relax—it's only *paan* juice. Different kinds of *paan* have different properties. It is basically meant as a digestive, but there are myriad add-ons, one of which is said to result in the *paan* becoming an aphrodisiac called a *palang tod* (bed-breaker). After eating this *paan,* your performance is said to become so athletic that it quite reduces the bed to smithereens. In less ambitious forms, the *paan* is a leaf wrapped around some betel nut. Try it at the **Gama Paan Shop** or the **Kuber Paan Shop** in the Godaulia area.

TOUR 9

CALCUTTA

Calcutta is an international symbol for urban collapse. Its most recent Nobel Laureate is Mother Teresa. Yet Calcutta harbours some of India's greatest artists and writers and a vibrant film industry. These sensitive folk swear they would die if they had to leave the city. As you spend time here, Calcutta will reveal an attraction, a commitment to culture and causes, and a vibrant identity that no other city in India has.

Suggested Schedule	
08:00	Breakfast at Flury's Tea Room in Park Street.
09:00	Most of Calcutta's monuments don't open until 10:00. Use the time until then observing the city. Go to the Maidan or take a Metro train ride, a good way to feel the city's pulse.
10:00	Visit Victoria Memorial, the 'Taj Mahal' of the British Raj.
11:30	Visit St. Paul's Cathedral, close to Victoria Memorial. Built in 1847, it is one of the best-known churches in India.
12:00	Visit the Indian Museum, the largest museum on the subcontinent, on Chowringhee (Jawaharlal Nehru Road) quite close to St. Paul's.
13:00	Lunch.
14:00	Drive down to Saheed Minar, Eden Gardens, BBD Bagh Area to Howrah Bridge (Rabindra Setu) over the river Hooghly.
15:30	Leave for the airport.
17:30	Depart from Calcutta.
19:35	Arrive in Madras. Check into hotel.

Calcutta

Once the capital of British India, Calcutta was a busy commercial centre and port, and with time it became a seat of culture and learning. Its commercial activity was matched by equally intense intellectual and cultural growth. The first modern Indian social reform movements started here. So did much of the impetus for India's independence from the British. India's Nobel Laureate in literature, Rabindranath Tagore, worked here. Even when the

British shifted the political capital back to Delhi, Calcutta remained the cultural, intellectual and commercial capital of India.

Today Calcutta is the largest city in India. Its port is among the busiest in the East. Thickly populated, Calcutta repels physically but attracts because of its distinct vitality. The great flowering of Indian thought and art started here, a fact of which the people of Bengal are immeasurably proud and whose glory the rest of India is fed up with hearing about. Many claim that Calcutta rests on its laurels and is today a dying city. Yet, amidst the dirt and filth, the spirit of the city lives on. In the dirtiest lanes you find a Mother Teresa; in dark corners people with barely enough to eat study philosophy and discuss politics. Poverty is around, yet Calcutta's clerks have been known to save their pennies until they have enough money to publish a volume of verse. It's a city of contradictions, of complexities, but above all, alive and pulsating.

The city has a population of around nine million. Situated a mere 6.4 metres above sea level, Calcutta lies along the east bank of the river Hooghly, a tributary of the Ganga. The city sprawls north/south along the river, and new localities like Salt Lake City have come up on the northeast of Calcutta. Languages commonly spoken in Calcutta are Bengali, English and Hindi. Durga Puja, during October and November, is the biggest festival. Calcutta has a large Christian population and both Christmas and New Year are celebrated with gaiety as the city dresses up for the season with baubles and trees, Santa Claus and carols. A never-to-be-forgotten experience is meeting a brown Santa in a red cotton dressing gown, singing 'Silent Night' in a Bengali accent on a humid afternoon.

Most of Calcutta's streets and roads have new names but are better known by their former names, causing hideous confusion to a newcomer to the city. The cause is not sadism, but nationalism. Since the streets were named after British rulers, after independence it was felt inappropriate to continue with them. Only on one occasion was there genuine mischief, when during the Vietnam war the local democratically elected Communist government decided to strike a blow for the brave Vietnamese by renaming Shakespeare Sarani (Road) as Ho Chi Minh Street. Since this street also rejoiced in the presence of the American Consulate, it was an acute embarrassment for the CIA types to admit the address of their workplace. (The local populace, the most left-wing in India, having elected a Communist government to power for several years running, are nevertheless lovingly loyal to the names of imperialists and still call the streets by their old colonial names.)

BBD Bagh (old Dalhousie Square) is named after three martyrs

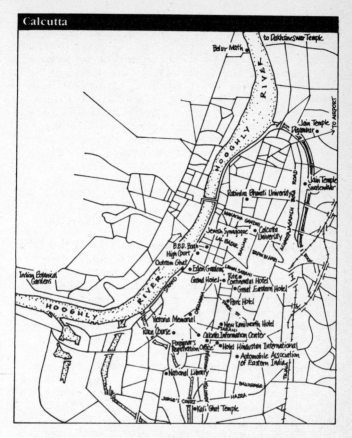

of Bengal — Benoy, Badal and Dinesh. This area is the seat of
commercial activity, and many private and government offices,
including the Calcutta High Court, are located here. The General
Post Office and the Reserve Bank of India are on the western side
of BBD Bagh. The entire northern side is dominated by the
Writers' Building, so named because it was originally built to
accommodate the writers (clerks) of the East India Company. The
West Bengal State Tourist Office (tel. 238271) is also in the BBD
Bagh area.

Coming southward from BBD is the Maidan (a huge park) and
the Chowringhee area. Central Calcutta is best viewed in
perspective around the rolling green lawns of the Maidan, three
square km of parkland dotted with trees and criss-crossed by
roads. At the southern end of the Maidan is the Calcutta Race
Course. Across the Maidan is Ochterlony Monument (Shaheed

Minar), a 48-metre-high column built in honour of the British General David Ochterlony. Chowringhee runs along the eastern side of the Maidan. Most of the budget hotels in Calcutta as well as some of the five-star hotels like the Oberoi Grand, and many airline offices, are located in and around Chowringhee.

New Market (Hogg Market), which was recently burnt down but is now being rebuilt, is close to Chowringhee. It is a very popular shopping area where you can get anything from a pine to an elephant (in case you suddenly feel the need to own one). There are a number of new air-conditioned markets in Calcutta. The Central Cottage Industries Emporium in Russel Street has a lot of interesting things to offer. Calcutta is well known for delicately embroidered linen, cotton wear and painted clay plaques.

Park Street, off Chowringhee, is Calcutta's most fashionable street, often compared to Oxford Street in London. It forms the main artery and is joined by several smaller streets on both sides. A little further down you'll find a cemetery. If you're British you may well discover an ancestor who was vanquished by India's main weapons against the British — cholera and malaria. Calcutta is dotted with such places. A vast number of Englishmen came to India to loot the country (with great success, it must be added) and Calcutta is littered with hidden houses, plaques to General this and writer that, and other reminders of 200 years of British rule.

To the east of Park Street are Ballygunj and several other of Calcutta's residential areas. Tollygunj in South Calcutta is the 'Hollywood of Eastern India' with a number of studios. Calcutta makes a number of feature films every year, mostly in Bengali.

Transport

A number of flights connect Calcutta's Dum Dum Airport to the rest of India. (The infamous Dum Dum bullets derived their names from an ordinance factory set up here during the Second World War.) The National Arrivals Lounge has a Tourist Information Centre (tel. 572611 ext. 440) and a Hotel Reservations counter as well. The regular airline coach service to the city stops at various hotels and terminates at the city airlines office (fare Rs 13). There are metered yellow-top and yellow taxis available at the airport. The fare to the city is around Rs 50 (£2). Yellow-top taxis are authorised to go outside the metropolitan area into the suburbs. The airport is 18 km from the city.

The Indian Airlines city office (tel. 260730 or 263390) is in Chittaranjan Avenue. The Government of India Tourist Office (tel. 443521 is in Shakespeare Sarani off Park Street. The railway station is at Howrah, across the river Hooghly on the west bank.

In addition to the Metro and the city bus service, Calcutta has

a tram service. Minimum fare is 40 paise. Yellow-top taxis charge
Rs 3.50 for the first 2 km and Rs 1.70 for every subsequent km.
Auto rickshaws operate mostly in the southern parts of Calcutta.
A unique feature of Calcutta is the use of hand-pulled rickshaws,
somewhat unusual for a big city, much like the trishaws you see
in Hong Kong or Singapore. The government is now trying to
introduce cycle rickshaws, but the current vehicle is most useful
for short distances through narrow streets. During peak hours,
when traffic is an utter mess, the rickshaw pullers can manoeuvre
their way through. Tariff is negotiable, but nearly the same as
taxis.

The buses during rush hour are a wondrous sight. Not only are
they enveloped completely by humanity but there are people
hanging outside the buses, with still more people hanging onto
them.

Sightseeing Highlights

▲▲▲**Victoria Memorial** — Planned by Lord Curzon as a
memorial to Queen Victoria, it was opened by the Prince of
Wales in 1921. Situated on the Calcutta Maidan, the memorial is
beautifully laid out with trees, pools and lawns all around. It
houses an art gallery, a portrait gallery and an interesting
museum. Don't miss the Old Calcutta picture gallery on the first
floor — it is fascinating how Calcutta grew over the centuries.
Open daily 10:00-17:00, closed on Mondays, entry Rs .50.

▲▲▲**Indian Museum** — Known also as Jadu Ghar (Magic
House), the museum houses an outstanding collection of
archaeological and anthropological exhibits. The Indian Museum
was founded in 1814 on the formal proposal of a Danish botanist.
The imposing building which houses the present museum was
constructed in 1875. It comprises six sections — Art,
Archaeology, Anthropology, Geology, Zoology and something
called Economic Botany. Each section has a wealth of exhibits.
The Art Gallery has an impressive collection. Art students sit in
corners busily sketching or painting. The museum is a convenient
walk from Sudder Street, Chowringhee or Park Street. Open
10.00-17:00, closed on Mondays, Entry Rs .50, free on Fridays.

▲▲**St. Paul's Cathedral** — Built in 1847 in the Gothic style,
St. Paul's stands to the east of Victoria Memorial. The spire of
the Cathedral rises 61 metres high. There are two beautiful
Florentine frescoes inside.

▲▲**Chowringhee & Maidan** — Standing parallel to each other,
you can't really miss these two Calcutta sights. Chowringhee, the
busy thoroughfare right in the city centre, reflects the
cosmopolitan character of the city. The Maidan is 3 square km of
vast green spaces characterised by a variety of zestful activities —
games, joggers, snake charmers, monkey and bear performers, as

well as political gatherings. From the Maidan you can see the
shimmering line of buildings of Chowringhee. Here you are away
from the crowds, yet not totally away from them. Not that you
can ever get completely away from crowds in Calcutta. Situated
on the Maidan is Shaheed Minar, known earlier as Ochterlony
Monument. In the northwest corner of the Maidan are the lovely
Eden Gardens, with a stadium which can accommodate 70,000
people. The football and cricket matches held here are legendary
for their noise and the passions they arouse.

▲▲**Howrah Bridge (Rabindra Setu)** — Try to see this, for
Calcutta is inconceivable without it. A miracle of engineering
skill, this huge cantilever bridge is supported by two piers 270 ft.
high from road level. Howrah bridge came into being in 1943.
Until then the Hooghly River was crossed by a pontoon bridge.
The span of the bridge between the piers is 1500 feet, the bridge
is 71 feet wide and almost perpetually jammed with traffic.

Accommodation

Hotel Oberoi Grand (tel. 290181), **Hindustan International**
(tel. 442394) and **Great Eastern** (tel. 232331) are some of
Calcutta's leading five-star hotels. Of the lesser hotels, **Fairlawn
Hotel** (tel. 244460) on Sudder Street is a landmark, with singles
at Rs 350 (£14) and doubles at Rs 450 (£18). Tariff includes all
meals and morning and afternoon tea. Mr. Smith, a Briton, and
his Armenian wife, run this establishment in a huge 200-year-old
building. A popular hotel, it is frequented by many, including
film stars from Bombay.

Lytton Hotel (tel. 291875/9), adjacent to Fairlawn, has singles at
Rs 330 (£13.20) and doubles at Rs 450 (£18). **Astoria Hotel** (tel
241359), again on Sudder Street, has rooms at RS 200 (£8).
Sudder Street has some cheaper hotels as well. **Hotel Diplomat**
(tel. 242145) has singles at Rs 60 (£2.40) and doubles at Rs 70
(£2.80), all with attached baths. **Shilton Hotel** (tel. 243613) on
Sudder Street is a large, dilapidated building, but rooms are
comfortable, priced at Rs 60 (£2.40) single, Rs 90 (£3.60) double.

The YMCA and YWCA in Calcutta offer excellent
accommodation. The **YMCA Chowringhee** (tel. 292192) has
singles at Rs 150 (£6) and doubles at Rs 200 (£8). The **YWCA
International Guest House** (tel. 297033), in Middletown Row
off Park Street, has singles at Rs 50 (£2) and doubles at Rs 60
(£2.40), but with common baths.

In the budget range a popular place is the **Salvation Army
Guest House** (tel. 242895) opposite Fairlawn Hotel on Sudder
Street. Run by missionaries, it has rooms from Rs 35 (£1.40) to
Rs 60 (£2.40) and the dormitory has beds at Rs 13 (£0.50) each.
There are a number of other guest houses and hotels offering
budget accommodation. The **Youth Hostel** is in Howrah, quite

far from the city. The government **Tourist Bungalow,** with doubles at Rs 40 (£1.60), is far away in Salt Lake City. The distance from the city is its biggest drawback. The airport has sleeping rooms at Rs 55 (£2.20) single, Rs 75 (£3) double.

Food

Calcutta has a number of excellent western style restaurants on Park Avenue including **Mocambo, Kwality, Trincas, Blue Fox** and **Skyroom.** Some have live bands. The five-star hotels have restaurants, coffee shops and bars.

Amber Restaurant (tel. 233477 or 236746 for reservations), behind Great Eastern Hotel, serves excellent Indian and Continental food. Though Amber occupies three floors, you may have to wait for a table if you go without a reservation. For vegetarian food, **Vineet** in Shakespeare Sarani is a good place. **Thandai** in Camac Street serves delicious traditional Indian cold drinks. Calcutta has a large Chinese population, and small Chinese restaurants can be found throughout Chinatown.

Bengali cuisine is very well known for its special preparations, particularly a wide variety of fish. Some restaurants include Bengali food on their menu, but for reasonable prices and real Bengali flavour, visit a small eating place called **Suruchi** at 89 Elliot Road. Run by the All Bengal Women's Union Home (a charitable organisation), Suruchi's chief claim to fame is its fresh-water fish preparations. Try the shellfish baked inside tender coconut, steamed mustard fish and the fish in rich yogurt sauce. You can have their economy meal — a *thali* for only Rs 8 — or try their special fish lunch for Rs 20.

Another Calcutta speciality is *kathi-kabab*, meat rolled in flaky *parathas* (fried bread). This is basically a Muslim preparation. **Nizam's,** near New Market, has been known for years for its excellent variety of *kathi-kababs*.

TOUR 10

MADRAS

South of the Vindhya Mountains lies another world. The culture, cuisine, traditions, languages and even appearance of the people are different. So is their habit—unique in the world—of shaking their heads side-to-side when they mean 'yes' and nodding up-and-down when they mean 'no'. But very few heads will go up and down for you, because the south is generally believed to be much friendlier than the north and its people more honest (though I'm not advising you to put this to the test).

Suggested Schedule

7:30	Depart on day trip to Kanchipuram and Mahaballipuram.
18:00	Return from your trip. Dinner.

Madras

Madras will be your first encounter with South India. The capital of the state of Tamil Nadu, Madras lies on the coast and is a major port. What were a few scattered villages about 350 years ago have today grown into the fourth largest city in India, with a population of over 3.25 million.

Madras was Britain's first major settlement in India. As a consequence, the city has great significance in British-Indian history. A fascinating amalgam of ancient, colonial and modern, Madras has managed to retain strong traditions that are evident in the people's love and understanding of all that constitutes South Indian heritage, such as certain kinds of music, dance and architecture. They are also very tradition-bound and conservative.

If you've got used to North India, Madras will present a culture shock. It's so totally different, yet so totally Indian, that the contrast strikes you immediately. Just as you feel you understand India, you come down south to find that there's an entirely new experience to wonder at.

Languages commonly spoken in Madras are Tamil and English. In case you've perfected your Hindi, it's quite useless here. In fact, Hindi is regarded in Madras the way the French regard the English language, so if you test out a few Hindi words all you'll get is a blank look and a higher price on whatever you're bargaining for. If you find South Indian names impossibly tongue-twisting compared to the shorter names of the north, console yourself—North Indians find them nearly as difficult and take frequent recourse to abbreviating them abruptly. So

Tiruchirapally becomes Trichy and Vishakapatnam is Vizag.

Geographically, the most prominent feature of Madras is the north-south Marina Beach, said to be the second-longest in the world. It runs from the harbour in the north to the cathedral in the south, a length of about 11 km. You'll find quite a profusion of Christian monuments all over the south (and wherever else the British went, since they believed it was God's wish that they convert the heathens while looting them).

The city itself can be divided into two parts. The older section is west of the dock area and north of Poonamallee High Road. This is the more congested part of the city, with lots of offices and local markets. A prominent landmark of the old city is Parry's Corner, which runs alongside the High Court Building. There is a fascinating flower and fruit market here.

A draw for locals and tourists alike is the Burma Bazaar, about five hundred little shops running along the road opposite the bus stands. In the evenings the bazaar is lit up and anything from modern electronics to the latest bestseller can be bought. Here as elsewhere bargaining is a must, though in Madras it's far more sophisticated than the more robust agonising, shrieking and beating of breasts in the North.

Lately, a number of slums have sprung up in the heart of the city, presenting a sharp contrast of haves and have-nots.

South of the Poonamallee High Road is the modern part of the city. Anna Salai Road, popularly known as Mount Road, the main artery here, commences from Fort St. George and passes through important shopping and business centres, banks and tourist and airline offices. Commander-in-Chief (C-in-C) Road, which branches off from Mount Road, has a number of deluxe hotels and restaurants. For shopping enthusiasts, Madras is famous for its silk and diamonds. The State Handicraft Emporium, Lepakshi, is in Mount Road.

Madras is a big film production centre, and all over the city you are confronted with huge, garish film billboards and cutouts. These you may appreciate with relish. You will find women with bosoms reminiscent of Mount Everest and thighs the size and shape of the Empire State Building. In fact, one memorable heroine was known as 'Thunder Thighs'. The Indian ideal of womanhood is a great deal more robust than the skinny clotheshorses of Paris. In a land where so many people are underfed, being even more underfed is not regarded as alluring. These film billboards are violently visible all over India, unashamedly hideous, and in Madras they have achieved the status of an art form. Recently there was one so long, so lurid, with the heroine so undressed, that it caused accidents on the streets and the courts had to be invoked to remove it.

While in Madras, pick up a copy of *Hallo Madras*, a booklet

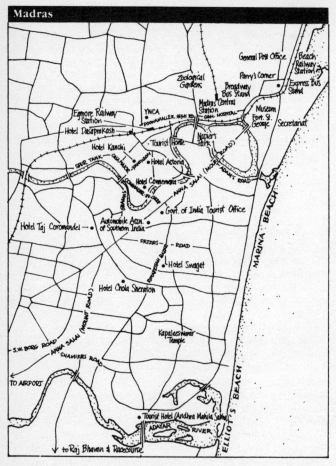

Madras

brought out every month containing useful information about the city, price Rs 3. The Kennedy Book House (tel. 81797) in Mount Road always keeps some copies of the latest edition in stock.

Transport

Madras has a domestic as well as an international airport, both with modern facilities (though Heathrow they're not). The domestic airport is connected by a regular coach service to the city airlines office, about 17 km away. Fare is Rs 20. Metered taxis, also available at the airport, charge about Rs 40 (£1.60) to the city centre. The Tourist Office has a counter at the airport (tel. 431686) which is open round the clock.

Madras has two main railway stations, Egmore and Central.
Both are close to Poonamallee High Road. The **India
Government Tourist Office** (tel. 88685-6) and the **Tamil
Nadu Tourist Office** (tel. 840752) are both in Mount Road,
quite close to each other. The **Indian Airlines** office (tel.
848711-2) is in Marshal Road, off C-in-C Road. The GPO,
Tamil Nadu State Transport (tel. 512011) bus stand and the
privately-run **Triuvalluvar Transport Corporation** (tel.
561835) are all located in the old city.

For local transport, yellow-top taxis, auto rickshaws and cycle
rickshaws are available. Taxis charge Rs 3 for the first 1.6 km
and Rs 1.70 for every subsequent km. Auto rickshaws charge Rs
2 for the first 1.6 km and Rs 1.20 for every subsequent km.
Cycle rickshaw rates are negotiable. A cycle rickshaw from Parry's
Corner to Mount Road will be about Rs 5. City buses are
frequent but crowded, minimum fare Rs.40.

Sightseeing Highlights

You have one full day in Madras, and we strongly recommend a
one-day trip to Mahaballipuram and Kanchipuram. The trip is
organized by Tamil Nadu Tourism (TNT) as well as by India
Tourism Development Corporation (ITDC). The TNT trip leaves
daily at 06:45 from their office on Mount Road and returns at
18:00 hrs. Since you reach Madras late in the evening, there will
be no time for advance bookings, so try the TNT trip first,
failing which try for a seat on the ITDC coach. Buses leave
frequently for Mahaballipuram and Kanchipuram from the Tamil
Nadu and Triuvalluvar bus stands. But it is advisable to take a
conducted trip on the TNT or ITDC service which have guides
on board. Tariff for both conducted trips is Rs 60 (£2.40) (non-
air-conditioned) or Rs 90 (£3.60) (for the air-conditioned coach).
▲▲▲**Mahaballipuram**—58 km south of Madras on the shore
of the Bay of Bengal, Mahaballipuram was once a thriving port of
the Pallava kings who ruled here around the 7th century AD.
Today it is a small village and a popular tourist destination. The
Pallavas built impressive monuments here, the best known being
the Shore Temple. Some of the most fascinating sculptures and
stone carvings can be seen in Mahaballipuram. There are nine
rock-cut cave temples, depicting scenes from Hindu mythology.
The world's largest stone bas-relief, measuring 27 metres by 9
metres, is another pride of Mahaballipuram. This huge whale-
back shaped rock faces the sea and is split with a fissure in the
middle.

The **Shore Temple,** constructed in the Dravidian style, has
two shrines facing east and west, dedicated to Lord Shiva and
Vishnu. A little way away from the Shore Temple are the famous
rathas (chariots). Five monolithic *rathas* are believed to have been

carved out of a single rock formation. Another interesting place in Mahaballipuram is the **Tiger's Cave**, 5 km away, an open-air theatre where cultural programmes were once held for the royal family.

The Mahaballipuram-Kanchipuram trip also includes a visit to **Thirukkalikundram**, 14 km away from Mahaballipuram. A famous pilgrim centre, it has an ancient Shiva temple and another hilltop temple. Around noon every day two birds, believed to be sacred, land on the hilltop temple and are fed by the priest. Legend has it that these birds are Lord Shiva and his consort Parvati, who come all the way from Varanasi to be fed in this temple.

▲▲▲**Kanchipuram**—Located 65 km west of Mahaballipuram, and 76 km from Madras, this is one of the seven sacred cities of India. It was successively the capital of the Pallavas, the Cholas and the rulers of Vijaynagar. During the 6th and 7th centuries AD, some of the best temples were built here. Some temples date back to the 4th century AD. Kanchipuram has also been a seat of learning. Kanchipuram is justly famous for its hand-woven silk fabrics. Some of the well-known temples in Kanchipuram are Kailasantha Temple, Vaikuntaperumal Temple and Ekambaresh Temple. Each temple has a distinct style and character and is easier to visit than to pronounce.

Accommodation

Reasonably priced hotels can be found in any part of Madras. The very cheap hotels are in the Parry's Corner area, most of them located in narrow streets in very congested areas, and are not recommended. Another disadvantage is the distance from here to the Mount Road area where tourist and airline offices are located.

In Irwin Road, opposite the Egmore station, are a number of clean, comfortable budget hotels. The **Chandra Lodge** (tel. 568863) has singles at Rs 55 (£2.20) and doubles at Rs 90 (£3.60), all with attached baths. **Hotel Vaigi** (tel. 567373) is a big multi-storey hotel at one end of Irwin Road which has only double rooms costing Rs 95 (£3.80) (non-air-conditioned) and Rs 190 (£7.60) (air-conditioned).

A fifty-year-old hotel in this area, recently renovated, is the **Hotel Impala** (tel. 561778) with singles at Rs 25 (£1) and doubles at Rs 45 (£1.80), all with attached baths. The rooms are tiny but adequate. The **Roseland Lodging House** close to the Impala has singles at Rs 25 (£1) and doubles at Rs 50 (£2), but with common bathrooms. **Tourist Homes (P) Ltd** (tel. 567080) right opposite Egmore Station has 36 rooms, all doubles, at Rs 80 (£3.20) with attached baths.

The **YWCA International Guest House** (tel. 39920), a lovely sprawling place in Poonamallee High Road, accepts both male and female guests. Tariffs, including breakfast, are singles Rs 60 (£2.40), doubles Rs 90 (£3.60) (twin sharing is Rs 30 (£1.20) per person in a double room). The **YMCA Guest House** (tel. 32831), with 12 double rooms all with attached baths at Rs 40 (£1.60), is at 74, Ritherdon Road. Dormitory charges here are Rs 15 (£0.60) per bed. Close by is the **Red Shields Salvation Army Guest House** (tel. 31821) in Vepery Road, which has doubles for Rs 40 (£1.60) (with attached baths) and Rs 25 (£1) (with common baths), and a dormitory charging Rs 10 (£0.40) per bed. The **Youth Hostel** (tel. 412882) has dormitory accommodation at Rs 7 (£0.30) per bed, but it is located in Indira Nagar, at a great distance from the city centre.

Around Mount Road, **Hotel Kanchi** (tel. 471100) in C-in-C Road is a deluxe hotel with singles for Rs 90 (£3.60) and doubles for Rs 125 (£5). Rooms with air-conditioners cost a little more. The hotel facilities include lockers, laundry, piped music, restaurants and a bar. The Indian Airlines office and the Government Tourist Office are a ten-minute walk from here.

Opposite the Star Cinema, about 15 minutes' walk from Marina Beach, is the **Broadlands Lodge**, in operation for the past 36 years. Housed in a well-maintained 100-year-old building, with lots of greenery and potted plants, it is under the personal supervision of the proprietor, Mr. A. P. Kumar. Singles and doubles with attached baths are Rs 35 (£1.40) and Rs 65 (£2.60) respectively. With common baths they are five rupees cheaper. Rooms are small but clean and very well-ventilated, with running water throughout the day. It's good value for money.

In addition to the above, Madras has the usual sprinkling of five-star hotels like the **Connemara, Adayar Park** and **Taj Coromandel**. The booklet *Hallo Madras* lists a number of hotels along with their tariffs.

Food

What you've called Indian food all your life is actually North Indian food. The South has a completely different cuisine. It doesn't have any curry to speak of, is much lighter on the stomach, and usually accompanied by a coconut chutney. *Idly* (pronounced 'edly', with the "e" as in 'empty') is rice compressed into a saucer shape. The *dosa*, a huge paper-thin rice pancake with a variety of fillings, is the most popular South Indian dish. It's a meal in itself. Ask for *masala dosa* which comes with a potato filling. A word of warning: if you thought North Indians had rotten table manners, the South Indians look as though they're squelching their food together to make mudballs. To acquaint yourself with a variety of South Indian preparations, try the buffet at **Hotel Connemara** (Rs 60) (£2.40). I suggest you turn vegetarian here. The vast majority of the population in the south is vegetarian, so the vegetarian food is much better than the non-vegetarian.

Another good place to eat is the **Yamuna Vegetarian Restaurant** in Mount Road. Here a 'Madras Meal'—a *thali*—comes for Rs 10. The menu lists ten types of *dosas*, or you can try the lemon rice or coconut rice. At Rs 3 a plate you get a large helping of either.

Dasaprakash in Poonamallee High Road is another popular place to try the local delicacies.

However, if you wish to try out a non-vegetarian meal, **Bukari Hotel** in Mount Road has excellent food. The restaurant at **Hotel Connemara** is also known for good seafood. In C-in-C Road, the **Mahal Restaurant** has *tandoori* preparations to offer. Next to the Mahal is the newly opened **Taco Tavern**, a Mexican takeaway. Dishes have exotic names like Bolita de Queso (cheese balls, Rs 14), God Father Pizza (Rs 12) or the Peperonata (macaroni, Rs 11.50). The food is good and service personalised, though it is doubtful whether Mexicans would find anything even remotely familiar about the food.

For non-vegetarian as well as vegetarian fast food, try the **Appointment** in C-in-C Road. The service is fast, and true to its name it helps you reach your appointment on time. Next to it is the **Shamiana Snack Bar**, a nice place for a quick bite.

For Chinese food try **Chunking** in Mount Road, or **The Golden Dragon** in Hotel Taj Coromandel which serves excellent food though it's on the expensive side.

Spencer's Building, a shopping complex in Mount Road, also has some good snack bars.

TOUR 11

TRIVANDRUM

Trivandrum is the capital of Kerala, a state with a profusion of green-capped mountains, palm-lined backwaters and luscious green paddy fields. It is also the state with the country's highest literacy rate, over 70%, which means nearly everybody speaks an incomprehensible form of English. Its people are some of the most successful in India in nearly every field, but their attitude toward the rest of mankind is best exemplified by the popular belief that their language, Malayalam, has no equivalent for the phrase, 'Thank you'.

Suggested Schedule	
05:00	Leave for airport.
06:35	Depart for Trivandrum.
08:35	Arrive in Trivandrum.
09:00	Check into hotel.
10:30	Catch a bus from the city bus stand for Cape Comorin (86 km away). Known as Kanya-kumari or Lands End, this is the southernmost tip of India and the point where three seas meet.
19:00	Return to Trivandrum. Dinner.

Trivandrum

Trivandrum has a population of about half a million. The best time to visit is October to March. It generally rains between June and September, and has a different charm—the rainswept countryside looks enchanting.

The city, spread over seven hills, sprawls in all directions, but the main area of activity is around Mahatma Gandhi Road (M.G. Road), which runs 2 to 3 km through the centre of the city. On the left of the northern end of M.G. Road, adjacent to the Mascot Hotel, is the Indian Airlines Office (tel. 66370). On the right, to the northern end of M.G. Road, is a complex comprising the Zoological Gardens, the Museum and the Art Gallery. Opposite this complex is the Kerala State Tourist Department office (tel. 61132). A little to the south is Trivandrum's Chandrasekharan Nair Stadium. Close to the stadium is the local bazaar, Connemara Market.

Midway along M.G. Road is the Secretariat and Statue Junction

area, around which a lot of budget hotel accommodation is
available. M.G. Road is a shopping area as well, and the State
Emporium, Kairali, has a branch at Statue Junction. Coir (made
from coconut husk) and cane products are a good buy in
Trivandrum. At the southern end of M.G. Road is the city
railway station (tel. 2287), opposite which are two bus stands—
one operating buses under the Kerala State Road Transport
Corporation and the other for the Tamil Nadu Transport
Corporation. These areas are incredibly noisy. The **Tourist
Reception Centre** (tel. 2643), which operates conducted
sightseeing trips in and around Trivandrum, is just outside the
bus stands. The Padmanabhaswamy Temple is close to the
railway station. Around this area, which is called the East Fort
area, are more hotels and restaurants, budget as well as more
expensive ones.

Trivandrum is fascinating. People even dress uniquely. In fact,
all over the South the men dress casually in a *lungi*, a sort of
sheet wrapped around the waist like a skirt. On particularly hot
days it's picked up from the bottom and tucked into the waist to
make a male mini baring hairy legs. The men are often bare-
chested, sensible given the humidity.

As you move around Trivandrum you will find temples,
churches and many mosques. All three religions—Hindu, Muslim
and Christian—have large followings here. There is general
prosperity both in the city and in the villages. Over the last
decade there has been a mass exodus of contract labour to the
Arab countries, and this has led to much prosperity in the region
and a change in the social system. The poor have become rich,
the people less conservative and far less willing to accept the
traditional caste groupings.

Languages commonly spoken in Trivandrum are Malayalam and
English.

Transport

At Madras Airport, ask for a window seat on your flight to
Trivandrum. Just before landing you get a fabulous view of the
lush green mountains and Kovalum Beach, as the aircraft flies
very low.

The airport is 7 km from the city. There are no trolleys, but
porters are available. The Tourist Information counter opens only
at 10:00, so predictably when you arrive it will be closed. There
is no coach service to the city. There is a local city bus service,
but you'll waste a lot of time looking for it. Take a taxi or an
auto rickshaw. Both are metered, but meters are rarely used in
Trivandrum. Airport-city journeys by taxi cost Rs 40 (£1.60) and
by auto rickshaw Rs 20 (£0.80). You can save by sharing the taxi
with others.

For local transport, there is a city bus service. The catch is that there are no numbers on the buses, and destinations are written only in the local language. The locals apparently don't believe—perhaps with good reason—that outsiders would want to use their local buses. You may as well use an auto rickshaw. It's not expensive, and saves time. The auto rickshaw drivers, however, drive like WWII kamikaze pilots who've just spotted the American fleet on the horizon. Some even have a song on their lips. There are no cycle rickshaws in Trivandrum.

Sightseeing Highlights

▲▲▲**Cape Comorin**—86 km from Trivandrum, Cape Comorin (commonly called 'C.C', also known as Kanyakumari) occupies a unique place among the tourist centres of India. It is the last spot on the land mass of India, where the waters of the Arabian Sea, the Indian Ocean and the Bay of Bengal meet. The three different colours are very distinct. Here the sun rises from the Bay of Bengal and sets in the Arabian Sea. Cape Comorin is also an important pilgrim centre, with legends connecting it to goddess Kanyakumari, a manifestation of Parvati, the consort of Lord Shiva.

The Kerala Tourist Department runs a daily one-day round trip to Cape Comorin, but it leaves at 07:30, while you reach Trivandrum later than that. But reaching C.C. independently is not much of a problem. From the Tamil Nadu bus stand there are three deluxe buses daily to C.C., one of them leaving at 10:30 hrs. Try to catch it. The fare is Rs 11 (about 45p) one way. From the Kerala bus stand, adjacent to the Tamil Nadu stand, there are buses to C.C. every half-hour. This bus stand is rather confusing and crowded at all times. For a ticket to Cape Comorin, go to Counter No. 1, next to the Kerala Tourist Information Counter at the bus stand. The one-way fare is Rs 6 for an ordinary and Rs 11.50 for a deluxe bus. The journey takes about 2½ hours through the beautiful countryside of Kerala and Tamil Nadu. From Cape Comorin to Trivandrum buses operate frequently until late in the night. The Cape Comorin bus stand is within walking distance of Land's End, where there are a Tourist Information Centre and a number of restaurants and shops.

Places of interest at C.C., all of them at Land's End, are:

Vivekananda Memorial—There are two rocks projecting out of the ocean. On one of these Swami Vivekananda, the great Indian philosopher, sat in deep meditation in 1892. It must have been uncomfortable, but it seemed to do him a lot of good, and on this rock stands the Vivekananda Rock Memorial, built in 1970, a blend of all the architectural styles of India and therefore an edifice that looks as if it was planned by an architect with a migraine. Here one can also see the footprints of the goddess

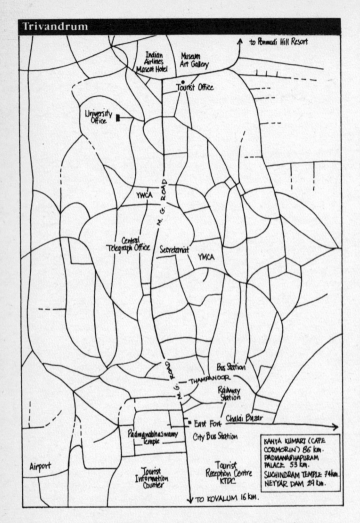

Trivandrum

Kanyakumari. (Your Western mind may wonder about these divine footprints and how we found out that they belonged to the goddess, but we of the spiritual East know best). There is a ferry service to reach the memorial. The return fare is Rs 3, entry ticket Rs 2. Remember to carry a pair of socks. You'll be asked to remove your shoes when entering the memorial, and the rock can be uncomfortably hot.

Kanyakumari Temple—Goddess Kanyakumari is said to have done penance here to win the hand of Lord Shiva as her husband, and the temple is dedicated to her.

Gandhi Memorial—Built on the spot where the urn
containing Mahatma Gandhi's ashes was kept for public viewing
before immersion into the sea in 1948, the memorial is an
architectural masterpiece. On every October 2nd (Gandhi's
birthday) the rays of the sun fall directly on the spot where the
urn was kept.

At Land's End there are rows of shops selling knick-knacks and
souvenirs, and also samples of the three different coloured sands
from the three seas.

If your departure for Goa is on a Monday, the flight will be
leaving at 12:30 hrs. Use the morning to sightsee in and around
Trivandrum. The following places are recommended:

▲▲▲**Kovalum Beach**—13 km away from Trivandrum, is an
especially pretty bay. The beach is lovely, though now often
crowded with tourists from all over the world. A particularly
large contingent of Russians are regularly brought here,
presumably because their government believes they will be safe
from temptation since even if they dash into the sea there's no
place to seek asylum within 3,000 miles. From the local city bus
stand at East Fort, you can share a taxi with other passengers and
pay Rs 10 single. From this stand there is also a bus every half-
hour to Kovalum, fare only Rs 1.40.

Zoological Park Complex—This comprises a beautiful zoo, a
museum with a good collection of bronzes and the Shri Chitra
Art Gallery, one of the best-maintained in India. It has copies of
the Rajput, Mughal and Tanjore schools, as well as some
fabulous originals of Raja Ravi Varma and Roerich, a Russian
painter who now lives in India and whose landscapes of the
Himalayas are magnificent.

Accommodation

Most restaurants in Trivandrum are called hotels, which can be
quite confusing. There are, however, a lot of genuine hotels
providing accommodation. The state government-run **Mascot
Hotel** (tel. 68990) is a lovely place with huge rooms and even
bigger bathrooms. The only health club in Trivandrum, Shilpa, is
located here.

On M.G. Road, close to the Indian Coffee House, the **YWCA
International Guest House** (tel. 77308) offers very comfortable
accommodation with attached bathrooms at Rs 40 (£1.60) single
and Rs 50 (£2) double. Guests of both sexes are welcome.

A little off M.G. Road, close to the British Council, is the
YMCA Guest House, which has very limited accommodation.
The British Council, incidentally, has a library and reading room
and a selection of British newspapers, so if you've been

completely starved of international news after a diet of single-mindedly insular Indian newspapers, you could dash in here for a while.

Hotel Luciya Continental (tel. 73443) at East Fort is considered one of Trivandrum's luxury hotels. Singles are Rs 125 (£5) and doubles Rs 175 (£7) for non-air-conditioned rooms. The Zodiac Restaurant here serves Indian, Chinese and Continental food and has a live band.

Near the station are a number of other hotels. **Arulakam** (tel. 79788) has singles for Rs 40 (£1.60) and doubles for Rs 60 (£2.40), all with attached baths. Singles with common baths cost only Rs 20 (£0.80). The **Sree Nivas Tourist Home** (tel. 79645), a big blue building near the bus stand, has singles for Rs 25 (£1) and doubles for Rs 40 (£1.60), all with attached baths. Singles with common bath cost only Rs 15 (£0.60). Rooms are adequate, but the area is crowded and noisy.

On M.G. Road opposite Ayurveda College is **Hotel Divya** (tel. 5339), a compact and clean place which only has doubles, Rs 60 (£2.40).

Around Statue Junction are a number of budget hotels. The **Mayfair Hotel** (tel. 76283) has comfortable rooms, singles for Rs 40 (£1.60) and doubles from Rs 50 (£2) upwards, all with attached baths. The **Shaji Tourist House** has rooms from Rs 50 (£2) upwards. **Hotel Pankaj** (tel. 76667), opposite the Secretariat, is a luxury hotel with singles at Rs 120 (£4.80) and doubles at Rs 150 (£6). The **MBR Tourist Home** has singles at Rs 20 (£0.80) and doubles at Rs 30 (£1.20), all with attached baths. The rooms are basic but okay. The **Swapna Tourist Home** (tel. 76891) again has functional rooms, all with attached baths, at only Rs 25 (£1).

Food

You will find all over India an item called by the uniquely contradictory name 'vegetable hamburger'. This is merely a mish-mash of assorted vegetables, largely the leftover potatoes from last night's dinner, bashed into a flat circle, then fried and served between a bun. This concoction is only eaten as a last resort—and this is likely to be the case now if you don't like coconuts, which Kerala food uses in every conceivable way. A typical Kerala meal consists of fish and coconut-based dishes with rice, the staple food. Rice is prepared in various ways—lemon rice, coconut rice, and a host of others.

Try a Kerala speciality, banana chips. Banana plantations are plentiful here and the bananas are cut, fried, dried, then salted as well as sweetened with a coating of jaggery (solidified molasses). Banana chips are a favourite with everyone and they're good to munch on long-distance trips.

South Indian coffee is rich, aromatic and strong. It's served
with a lot of milk and sugar, and has a very distinct flavour.
Those who have it become addicts and claim they can't touch any
other. Certainly it's a welcome change from the weak instant
mixture you get everywhere else in India.

The **Mascot Hotel** has a very fine restaurant with air
conditioning, first-class service, excellent food and reasonable
prices. Helpings are large. When eating there, try the coconut *nan*
(sweet bread) and the coconut soufflé. The Mascot also has a
barbecue next to the bar.

Nest, the coffee shop at Hotel Luciya Continental, has some
Kerala specialities and *thali* meals on its menu. **Indian Coffee
House** in M.G. Road, run by a cooperative society, is a well laid-
out place serving cheap vegetarian meals. The food is both greasy
and spicy. Nearby, the **Shri Durga** vegetarian restaurant is air-
conditioned and the quality of the food is much better. For fast
foods, try the **Sizzler** near the Kerala bus station. It offers a
variety of chicken preparations.

The air-conditioned **Safari Restaurant** in M.G. Road is a nice
place, with the Peeyush Bar attached to it. The **Roof Garden
Restaurant** is adjacent to the Indian Coffee House. The food is
quite cheap and not bad. There are also a number of other eating
places in M.G. Road.

TOURS 12 & 13

GOA

On the western coast, in the narrow strip of land between the
Arabian Sea and the Western Ghats, lies a strip of paradise called
Goa. It's a land of wide sandy beaches, sprawling rice fields and
lush green countryside. With its roots firmly entrenched in a rich
past of diverse cultures — Hindu, Muslim and Portuguese
Catholic — Goa has evolved into a strange admixture with its
own uniquely Latin character.

Suggested Schedule

Tour 12

08:00	Depart for airport. (If it happens to be a Monday, spend the morning at beautiful Kovalum Beach, 13 km from Trivandrum, or see the local sights of Trivandrum.)
09:10	Depart for Goa.
11:20	Arrive in Goa.
12:00	Reach Panjim, check into hotel.
14:00	Lunch.
15:00	Visit the popular Calangute Beach, referred to as the 'Queen of Beaches', 15 km from Panjim. Try Portuguese food at the restaurant O Coqueiro in Porvari, a village between Calangute and Panjim.
Evening	Take a stroll along the Mandovi River/18th June Road.

Tour 13

09:00	Join the South Goa conducted tour starting from the Tourist Hostel, Panjim.
18:15	Take a river cruise on the luxury launch *Santa Monica,* starting from Betim jetty opposite Mandovi Hotel.
Evening	Dinner. Try Chit Chat at the Tourist Hostel or the Riorico at the Mandovi Hotel for typical Goan food.

*NOTE: Indian Airlines flight 468 departs from Trivandrum at
09:10 and arrives at Goa at 11:20 hours every day except Monday.
On Monday, Air India flight 921 leaves Trivandrum at 12:30 and,
on its way to Kuwait and Dubai, arrives in Goa at 13:35 hrs. The
above schedule is based on IC flight 468.*

Goa was discovered by westerners during the 1960s when hippies stumbled onto it and found golden beaches, a blue sea and ridiculously low prices. Even the waving palms, for once in India, were vegetational rather than human. Even today the last of the hippies linger on, the women frequently topless and often as much a tourist attraction as the beaches. The natives are friendly, highly westernised, frequently Christian, and happily generous in sharing their *feni* (a foul-smelling but potent drink).

Goa

600 km south of Bombay, Goa has a population of about a million. It stretches north/south a length of 105 km, with some of the best beaches in the world. From east to west it is about 60 km, the entire land covered with verdant forests, coconut and cashew trees and mango groves interspersed with paddy fields for rice, the staple food of the people.

The Portuguese arrived in Goa in 1510 AD and ruled the land for 451 years until 1961 when India finally took over. Statehood was granted to Goa in May 1987, and it is the 25th and youngest state of India. Languages commonly spoken are Konkan, English and Marathi.

Three major communities — Hindu, Christian and Muslim — celebrate their festivals round the year in a remarkable spirit of joy and goodwill now that the Portuguese aren't there any more. Beautiful churches, temples and mosques dot the countryside. Some of the shrines of Goa are famous the world over for their antiquity, unique architectural style and as pilgrimage centres. Poets and travellers alike have lavished praise on Goa's scenic splendour. In 1983, when the leaders of the Commonwealth governments met in New Delhi, Goa hosted Mrs. Thatcher and others for a retreat after the meeting. The golden-hued beaches and Goa's charm could relax anyone, be it a head of government or an ordinary mortal who comes here to get away from the madding crowds.

Tourists flock to Goa throughout the year, but the best time to visit is between October and February. June to September is considered off-season because of the heat and the rains. However, many people believe that Goa is even more beautiful during the monsoons and certainly the sight of the endless and massive banks of black clouds rolling and thundering as they head into the country is awesome. The monsoons, though detested by tourists and tennis players, keep India alive.

Once a fishing village, Panjim (also called Panaji) is now the capital of Goa. Panjim is charmingly located along the left bank of the Mandovi River. There are beautiful red-roofed houses, built in the Latin style, and also many modern buildings, well-laid-out gardens, statues and tree-lined avenues.

The long bridge over the Mandovi River, connecting Panjim to
north Goa, collapsed in July 1986 and has since been under
repair. There is, however, a 24-hour ferry service to transport
people to and fro, which the state government is operating free of
charge until the bridge is back in operation. There are three main
ferry points for north Goa, two to transport passengers and one
that carries vehicles across the river. Dona Paula is connected by
a ferry service to Mormugao Harbour in south Goa.

The **Indian Airlines** office (tel. 3826, 3831) is in the Dempo
Building, quite close to the Mandovi Hotel and adjacent to the
Panjim local bazaar. Bookings for conducted tours and the river
cruise can be made at the **Tourist Hostel** on 31st January Road.
A walk from the airlines office to the Tourist Hotel takes less
than ten minutes. The **State Government Tourist Office** (tel.
5583) is at the Tourist Home at Patto, about five minutes' walk
from the Tourist Hostel. Between the Hostel and the Home is
Panjim's **General Post Office** (tel. 3704). Around Church
Square are the Alfonso de Albuquerque Road and the 18th June
Road, and along these two are located the top hotels, restaurants
and shopping areas of Panjim. All of the above-mentioned places
are within convenient walking distance from each other.

The **Youth Hostel** is about 3 km away from the Tourist
Hostel, close to Miramar Beach. This is the nearest beach to
Panjim, well-connected by the city bus service. The bus fare from
the Tourist Hostel to the Youth Hostel/Miramar Beach is 50
paise. A taxi would charge over Rs 10 to cover the distance. The
Kadamba bus stand, a ten-minute walk from the Tourist Hostel,
is fairly well organised. City buses as well as long-distance buses
and buses to south Goa and Old Goa operate from here.

Kala Academy, in Dayanand Bandodkar Marg about 2 km
from the Tourist Hostel, organises cultural dance and music
programmes from time to time. The Tourist Office keeps
information about their programmes.

Generally, Goa is friendly, informal, easy-going, and meeting
people is far easier and more rewarding than in most other places
in India which tend to be very closed. Do make an attempt to
meet the locals.

Transport

Goa's Dabolim Airport is 29 km from Panjim. A coach service,
operated at fixed times, connects the airport with the Indian
Airlines office at Panjim. The fare is Rs 20 (£0.80). Taxis charge
a flat rate of Rs 120 (£4.80) to the city. Share a taxi with other
passengers to cut costs. There is no official auto rickshaw stand at
the airport, but a cruising auto rickshaw can be hired for Rs 60
(£2.40). Yellow-top taxis and auto rickshaws in Goa are metered
but very rarely are the meters used. Generally a fixed fare is

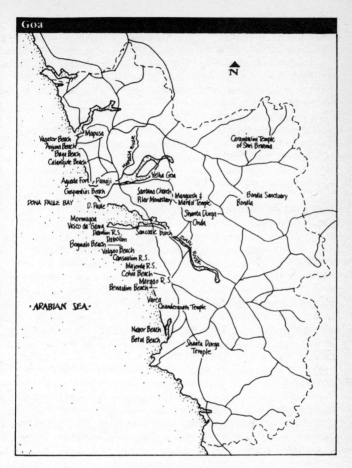

Goa

Vagator Beach
Anjuna Beach
Baga Beach
Calangute Beach
Mapusa
Mandvi River
Carambolim Temple
of Shri Bramha
Aguada Fort
Panaji
Gaspardias Beach
Velha Goa
Santana Church
Pilar Monastery
Manguesh &
Maruti Temple
Bondla Sanctuary
Bondla
DONA PAULE BAY
D. Paule
Shanta Durga
Onda
Mormugoa
Vasco da Gama
Dabolim R.S.
Dabolim
Bogmalo Beach
Sancoale Church
Zuari River
Velsao Beach
Consaulim R.S.
Majorda R.S.
Colva Beach
Margao R.S.
Benaulim Beach
· ARABIAN SEA ·
Varca
Chanderaneth Temple
Nabor Beach
Betul Beach
Shanta Durga
Temple

charged for point-to-point destinations. There are no trolleys at the airport, so make do with porters. The expected tip is about Rs 2 per piece of baggage. There is a small but helpful Tourist Information Centre (tel. 2644) at the airport. The nearest rail head is Margoa.

In Panjim, yellow-top taxis and auto rickshaws can be hired off the roads, and private tourist taxis from tour operators or from the **Travel Division,** Tourist Hostel (tel. 3396, 3903). Fixed taxi rates are: yellow-top taxis, Rs 3.50 for the first km and Rs 3 for every subsequent km; auto rickshaws, Rs 2 for the first km and Rs 1.75 per subsequent km. But these rates are almost never followed and a fixed fare must be paid. Going around in auto rickshaws and taxis can be very expensive in Panjim as there are no cycle rickshaws.

City buses are operated by the **Kadamba Transport Corporation** (tel. 5401) and also by private bus operators. Buses have destinations clearly written in front but they don't have any numbers. On private buses, no tickets are issued against the fare given to the conductor, which leads to rather rich bus conductors and rather poor bus owners.

The most exciting and best way to get around Goa is on a motorcycle. You can hire one for the day, complete with driver, and sit on the pillion behind him while he whizzes through traffic at breakneck speed. You can then hold your breath, say your prayers and, in between, admire the countryside. They are usually quite safe, though.

Sightseeing Highlights

South Goa Tour — Conducted daily by the Tourism Development Corporation (09:00-18:00 hrs, Rs 35 (£1.40)), the tour in a luxury coach covers important places in south Goa. There is a guide on board. The following places are included:

Old Goa Churches — 9 km from Panjim, at Old Goa, is a complex of ancient churches. Among the well-known Christian shrines here, the foremost is the Dom Jesus Basilica which houses the relics of St. Francis Xavier in a silver casket entombed in a marble mausoleum in the Florentine style interior. Some other churches are St. Cajetan Church, the Convent of St. Francis of Assisi and the Chapel of St. Catherine.

Shri Manguesh and Shantadurga Temples — The 400-year-old shrine of Shri Manguesh is dedicated to Lord Shiva. Ten kilometres from here is the Shantadurga temple with its beautiful inner sanctum where the deity is kept.

Margoa — The commercial centre of southern Goa, Margoa is linked by rail to the rest of India and on the National Highway with neighbouring states. Its ancient buildings and quaint architecture are reminders of the Portuguese past.

Colva Beach — Great scenery here. Sand, sea and sky blend in enchanting natural harmony.

Mormugao Harbour — One of the finest natural anchorages on the west coast of India and the hub of maritime activity. Passenger and cargo ships come and go from all over the world.

Vasco da Gama — A modern, well-laid-out city 4 km from Mormugao Harbour, with an interesting fish market.

Pilar Seminary — Important religious and educational centre for Christian missionaries. You may be tempted to join it, considering the magnificent panorama of the countryside and the fine view it commands of the Zuari River.

Dona Paula — An idyllic and picturesque picnic spot, with a beautiful statue of Dona Paula. The lagoon is a clear blue with

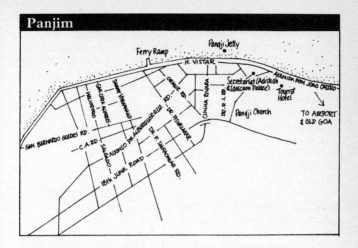

still, calm water. Dona Paula is a village where the lady of that name, the most famous of the Portuguese sirens, lived and died. The fishermen have a marvellous collection of ghost stories about Dona Paula and her lovers.

The town has facilities like boating and steamboat rides, as well as a fine view of Mormugao Harbour, which can be reached from here by ferry.

Miramar Beach — Only 4 km from Panjim, a lovely garden beach of soft sands girdled with palm trees. It's the closest beach to Panjim.

More Sightseeing Highlights

▲▲**River Cruise** — On the river Mandovi in Panjim, there are two daily cruises on a luxury launch, the *Santa Monica,* the first one from 18:00 to 19:00 hours and the second from 19:15 to 20:15 hrs, fare Rs 25 (£1). Food and drinks can be bought on board. A live music programme presents Goan and Portuguese music and colourful dances. Everyone gets into the mood and by the end of the trip you find yourself joining the dance. It's great fun. Carry a scarf, as it gets windy. The cruise offers a most relaxing evening. Don't miss it.

▲▲▲**Calangute Beach** — 15 km northwest of Panjim is the well-known Calangute Beach. A lovely Tourist Hostel overlooks the sea. There are music and dance competitions and beach shows. To get to Calangute Beach, cross the Mandovi River by ferry from Betim Jetty, then catch a bus that goes right to the beach. The bus takes 30 minutes and the fare is Rs 1.30.

▲▲**Fort Aguada Beach/Beach Resorts** — From Calangute, you can take a bus to Kandoli, then walk about 10 minutes to the absolutely gorgeous Fort Aguada Beach and Beach Resorts. The most expensive hotel in Goa, the Aguada Hermitage (tariff up to Rs 2500 (£100) per night), sits on this beach. The Commonwealth heads of government came here for their retreat, and no one in India believes they did any work at all.

Accommodation

If you're planning to visit Goa in December or January, reservations are advisable as these months see a huge influx of tourists to Goa. An estimated 775,000 people converge on the state, which is about three-quarters of a person for every inhabitant.

Hotel Fidalgo (tel. 6291, 6299) is Panjim's most prestigious hotel, with singles at Rs 525 (£21) and doubles at Rs 750 (£30). **Hotel Mandovi** (tel. 6270/79), one of Panjim's oldest luxury hotels, overlooks the river Mandovi and has single rooms at Rs 200 (£8) and doubles at Rs 400 (£16). Both hotels are centrally air-conditioned. **Hotel Sona** (tel. 4426 or 3488), near the GPO, is another large hotel with singles at Rs 95 (£3.80) and doubles at Rs 105 (£4.20). The **Tourist Hostel** (tel. 3396 or 3903), an imposing six-storey building, has singles at Rs 60 (£2.40) and doubles at Rs 75 (£3), all with attached baths.

The government **Tourist Home** (tel. 5583) and **Youth Hostel** (tel. 5433) have only dormitory accommodation at Rs. 10 (£0.40) per bed. There is another **Tourist Home** (tel. 3359), run privately, which only has double rooms at Rs 45 (£1.80), with bathrooms common to several rooms. The **City Guest House** (tel. 6005), very centrally located near the Secretariat building, has singles at Rs 25 (£1) and doubles at Rs 40 (£1.60), all with common baths. There are family rooms for Rs 60 (£2.40) with attached baths. **Keni's Hotel** (tel. 4581-86), close to Fidalgo, has singles at Rs 70 (£2.80) and doubles at Rs 120 (£4.80).

Around Church Square, close to the Tourist Hostel, a number of hotels provide accommodation between Rs 50 (£2) and Rs 100 (£4) per day. Some of them are: **Hotel Ambika** (tel. 4987), **Classic Hotel** (tel. 4075), and **Panjim Inn and Guest House** (tel. 4723). Some hotels with tariffs below Rs 50 (£2) are **Central Lodge** (tel. 4992), **Deluxe Lodge** (tel. 5037) close to the Tourist Hostel. **Mandovi Pearl Guest House** (tel. 3928) behind the Tourist Hostel, and **Hotel Republica** (tel. 4630) near the Secretariat.

Food

The best of Goan cuisine is non-vegetarian, specifically seafood. An exotic Goan dish is *shakuti*, a curry made of either chicken, lamb or turtle. It is pungent and generally eaten with rice. Other Goan specialities include *vindaloo* and *saurpatel*, both made with pork, mutton and liver. The typical Goan fish or prawn curry is delicious though pungent. Ask them to go easy on the chillies. Finish off with *bebinca,* a sweet dish prepared in coconut milk. Indian, Chinese and Continental food, as well as American fast food, are also available in Panjim.

For Goan food, **Rio Rico** at the Mandovi and **Chit Chat** at the Tourist Hostel are recommended. The restaurant at **Hotel Fidalgo** serves both Continental and Goan food. For Portuguese food, **O Corqueiro,** just a little way away across the Mandovi at Porvari, is the best bet. **Hotel Aroma** at Cunha River Road, Panjim, also has good Portuguese food.

For vegetarian South Indian food (in case you've become an addict) try the **Taj Mahal Restaurant** on Alfonso de Albuquerque Road. This Taj Mahal, of course, is no relation to the one in Agra. Pray refrain from tasteless jokes like whether Shah Jahan buried his queen in the kitchen; the waiters have heard them all.

Shalimar, close to this Taj Mahal, serves good Indian as well as Goan food. **Goenchin,** near 18th June Road, is well-known for Indian *tandoori* cuisine. The newly opened **Magabite** on 18th June Road is a lovely fast food parlour. The Mango Shake here, at Rs 5, will whet your appetite for another — it's delicious. At Church Square, another popular fast food place, the oddly named **Chicky Chocky** serves excellent pizzas. Visit **Megason's Delicatessen** ajdacent to Megason's fast food, and try out *bebinca.*

In Panjim, as in all of Goa, there are a number of bars. *Feni,* the popular local drink, is distilled either from cashew or from coconut, and is very, very potent. It smells disgusting.Cashew *feni* is a little like vodka, while coconut *feni* could be compared to gin. A milder variety of *feni* is called *urraca.* At any local bar, *feni* costs between Rs 3 and Rs 5 a peg. Matured cashew *feni* costs a little more. You can't have *feni* neat — it's awful. Mix it with orange squash or tomato juice to mask the smell and flavour, then rejoice in the consequences.

With your drink, try the local cashews with their tender skin on. They come in packs of two sizes, 200 grammes (Rs 16) and 400 grammes (Rs 32). These delicious cashews are a Goa speciality you won't find anywhere else in India.

TOURS 14 & 15

BOMBAY

After a relaxed break on the beaches of Goa, you land in
Bombay, a city with a population of over nine million. Talk of
culture shock!

Suggested Schedule

Tour 14

06:30	Reach the Indian Airlines office in Panjim to catch the coach or share a taxi to the airport.
08:25	Depart from Bombay (IC 164).
09:20	Arrive in Bombay.
10:00	Travel to city, check into hotel, lunch.
14:00	City sightseeing. The Maharashtra Tourism Development Corporation (MTDC) has a conducted afternoon sightseeing tour daily from 1400 to 1900 hrs, fare Rs 40 (£1.60), starting and ending at the MTDC city office at Nariman Point, covering Prince of Wales Museum, World Trade Centre, Gateway of India, Mani Vhavan, Hanging Gardens, Kamla Nehru Park, World Dairy, Nehru Science Centre and Taraporewala Aquarium.
Evening	Go to the theatre or see a Hindi film.

Tour 15

09:00	Visit the Elephanta Caves. Excursion starts from the Gateway of India.
13:00	Lunch.
Afternoon	See and feel the city on your own, not as part of a guided tour. Make it an early evening — your flight tomorrow morning leaves at 0615 hrs.

Bombay

Bombay is the capital of the state of Maharashtra. It is the New
York of India, the nation's financial and industrial capital and the
major centre for the arts, films and magazine publishing. Property
prices in South Bombay are as high as any Western city. Like
New York, Bombay is situated on an island and there just isn't
any land available, so Bombay builds upwards and the skyline at

night is a blaze of glittering skyscrapers. The island is located between Bombay Harbour and the Arabian Sea, running lengthwise from north to south. The airport is to the north, whereas the southern tip of Bombay is a mammoth commercial centre.

Bombay has an attraction for the poor that is proving nearly fatal to the metropolis. Thousands of job seekers and fortune hunters flock to the city every day, so it's bursting at the seams and services are at breaking point. Like Victorian London, people live in unimaginable squalor amidst some of the greatest wealth in India and even the world. Personal fortunes of tens of millions of pounds are quite common, as are small three-bedroom flats that sell for a quarter of a million pounds. The new rich are numberless in this city of go-getters. The even more numberless poor believe that they too can make it, or at least earn enough in Bombay to support their families back home in the village quite comfortably. Life is frenetic, loud, and the opportunities immense. Even the poorest Bombay-Wallah has a pride in being part of India's richest, most cosmopolitan, most expensive, most amazing city. English is commonly understood in Bombay. Popularly spoken languages are Marathi and Hindi.

English theatre in Bombay is very active. Look up the Theatre/Drama column in any local newspaper. The Government of India Tourist Office opposite Churchgate Station publishes a fortnightly information letter on dance, music and drama in the city. You might want to see a Hindi film just to find out what those garish hoardings are all about. Most Hindi films have music, dance, good guys, bad guys and fights. Kissing and nudity are not permitted, so directors are always experimenting with how close they can get two pairs of lips without meeting. Due to the nudity ban, actresses spend a lot of time falling into ponds and getting caught in rainstorms while wearing their flimsiest clothes. Bombay, the centre of the Hindi film industry, produces more film every year than Hollywood. There is also a small art film movement which makes excellent films everyone is very proud of and no one watches.

Given the size of the city, there are surprisingly few places to see. Most people enjoy it, however, for its sheer Bombay-ness — the diversity of people, the fast pace, the skyscrapers, the opportunities for a good time in complete anonymity, the openness of the lifestyles, the skyline at night and, of course, the sea which is always around you.

The Indian Airlines City Office (tel. 2021441, 2021626) is in the Air India Building at Nariman Point, and the airport coach service operates from here. The Maharashtra Tourism Development Corporation (MTDC), tel. 2026713, 2027762, is on Madame Cama Road, adjacent to Nariman Point. The city sightseeing tours operate from here. The Government of India Tourist Office (tel. 293144) is on Maharashi Karve Road opposite Churchgate Railway Station, which is about 15 minutes' walk from Nariman Point. The sea face from Nariman Point towards Churchgate and further on is called Marine Drive.

Madame Cama Road links Nariman Point to the Colaba area. Behind the Colaba shopping centre in the Apollo Bunder area are the Gateway of India and the Taj Mahal Hotel, both prominent landmarks of Bombay. Colaba has a number of budget hotels.

North of Colaba is the Fort area, also known as the Hutatma Chowk area. The Jehangir Art Gallery and the Prince of Wales museum are located here. The Fort is a busy commercial centre. The Handloom House is also located here. The Central Cottage Industries Emporium is in the Apollo Bunder area. On the walkways of the Fort area are a number of vendors selling anything from imported drinks and perfumes to electronic goods.

As you keep walking up the Fort area, you'll reach the Bombay Victoria Terminus ('V.T.') station, a neo-Gothic extravaganza inaugurated in 1887 to celebrate Queen Victoria's Golden Jubilee. The main feature is the central dome, bearing a 16½-foot-high figure of a lady holding a flaming torch pointing skyward to symbolise progress. A leisurely walk from the Gateway of India to V.T. will take about half an hour. The General Post Office, a massive building, is close to the V.T. station.

Marine Drive extends from Nariman Point to the Chowpatty Beach. Up north comes the Worli area and the Mahaluxmi Race Course. The suburbs of Mahim and Bandra are also to the north. The airport is close to the Juhu area. If you wish to visit the suburbs of Bombay, it is advisable to take a local train, which is much faster and cheaper than either a taxi or a bus.

Transport

Bombay has a very busy national airport, Santa Cruz, as well as Sahar International Airport. The two are a short drive from each other. The Indian Airlines city office is at Nariman Point in South Bombay, about 20 km from the airport. There is a half-hourly coach service between the airport and the city office and vice-versa. City-to-airport transport by coach is Rs 20 (£0.80). A taxi for the same distance will be from Rs 70 to Rs 80 (£2.80-£3.20). The pre-paid taxi counter at the airport is useful. You pay in advance at the counter and avoid the possibility of a fierce haggle afterwards.

There is a well laid-out local train system with three railway terminals. Churchgate and Victoria Terminus (V.T.) are toward South Bombay and Bombay Central, true to its name, is in central Bombay. Trains to the western suburbs operate from

Churchgate, and for the eastern suburbs from V.T. In addition to trains, the city bus service connects different parts of Bombay. Yellow-top taxis are easily available. Charges are Rs 3.75 for the first 1.6 km and additional fare according to the revised tariff card available from the driver. Generally the revised tariff is about four times what the meter shows.

Auto rickshaws ply only in the suburbs of Bombay. Horse-drawn carriages, known as Victorias, are available in South Bombay at places like Nariman Point and Colaba, but they are used for pleasure rides, not transport. A ride in a Victoria along Marine Drive is good fun, but they generally operate late in the evenings when there is less traffic on the roads. Fares are negotiable.

Accommodation

Bombay has plenty of accommodation to offer, yet all the places may be overbooked — such is the influx of people to this city. Lately a large number of Arabs have been visiting Bombay, especially during the monsoons to see the heavy showers which they've never seen back in their desert home.

There are a number of five-star hotels spread all over Bombay, like the **Oberoi Bombay and Oberoi Towers** (tel. 2024343) at Nariman Point, **Taj Mahal International Continental** (tel. 2023366) facing the Gateway of India, **Leela Penta** (tel. 6321126) and **Centaur** (tel. 6126660) close to the Bombay airport, **Sun and Sand** (tel. 571481) on Juhu Beach, **SeaRock** (tel. 6425454) at Bandra, **Hotel Ambassador** (tel. 2041131) near Churchgate Station, and **Hotel President** (tel. 4950808) in the Colaba area. There are three-star hotels all over the metropolis. A list of Bombay hotels is available at the tourist office.

The following are budget lodgings in Colaba, the central area close to the airline and tourist offices and banks. In Madame Cama Road adjoining Colaba is the **YWCA International Guest House** (tel. 2020445 or 2020598). Singles here are Rs 70 (£2.80) and doubles Rs 138 (£5.50), all well-furnished and with attached baths. Tariff includes breakfast. The YWCA has a pleasant staff and the rooms are well-maintained. There is a lounge with a TV which becomes a meeting place for residents in the evenings. Ensure accommodation by advance booking with a money order for one night's tariff to the Manager, YWCA International Guest House, 18 Madame Cama Road, Bombay.

The **YMCA Guest House** in Bombay is near the Bombay Central Station, quite a distance from Colaba. The tariff is the same as the YWCA. There is a **YMCA Hostel** in Colaba in Cooperage Road, but it is for students only and doesn't take tourists.

The **Salvation Army Red Shields House** (tel. 241824) is at

30 Mereweather Road, behind Hotel Taj Mahal. Captain Parkhe, the manager, runs the place very efficiently. There are ten rooms here, singles for Rs 100 (£4) and doubles for Rs 200 (£8), all with common baths. The tariff includes all three meals. The dormitory costs Rs 50 (£2) per day, again including all meals. There are a dining hall, a lounge and a library. Men and women are accommodated on separate floors. Checkout time is 9 am.

Walking down Mereweather Road, you'll find some more budget hotels and guest houses just opposite the Salvation Army one. At 35 Mereweather Road is **Jones Lodging House** (tel. 240031) in the Abbas building. Here singles are Rs 40 (£1.60) with attached baths and doubles Rs 60 (£2.40) with a common bath. The dormitory has beds for Rs 25 (£1). The amenities are basic. **Carlton Hotel** (tel. 2020642) is at 12 Mereweather Road, with singles for Rs 50 (£2) and doubles for Rs 100 (£4), all with common baths. Another popular place at 41 Mereweather Road is **Whalley's Guest House** (tel. 221802). All rooms are with common baths, singles for Rs 77 (£3.10) and doubles for Rs 145 (£5.80). The tariff includes breakfast. Run by Mrs. Satyani, it is an efficiently managed place.

Hotel Rex and **Stifles** (tel 230960) at 8 Ormiston Road, again behind the Taj Mahal Hotel, have been popular places with tourists for a long time, though now the service has deteriorated and the tariff has also gone up. Both hotels belong to one man but are under separate management. Rex is on the third and fourth floors, while Stifles is on the first and second floors. Tariff for both is Rs 116 (£4.65) for singles and Rs 155 (£6.20) for doubles, all with attached baths.

Hotel Cowles (tel. 240232) at 15 Watton Road, Colaba, has singles for Rs 136 (£5.45) and doubles for Rs 185 (£7.40), all with attached baths, non-air-conditioned. Tariff includes breakfast. The hotel has a total of 39 rooms and has been in operation for 36 years. Mr. Moolchandani, the proprietor, takes personal care and interest in his guests.

Another popular hotel in Colaba, not budget but two-star, is **Hotel Godwin** (tel. 241226) in Garden Road. There are 38 rooms in total, all air-conditioned, with singles at Rs 315 (£12.60) and doubles at Rs 410 (£16.40).

The **Gateway Hotel** (tel. 235114) in Apollo Bunder next to Taj Mahal Hotel, has air-conditioned double rooms at Rs 220 (£8.80) per day. Also in Apollo Bunder is **Hotel Prosser's** (tel. 241715) with singles for Rs 100 (£4) and doubles at Rs 120 (£4.80), all with common baths. The rooms are far from clean and the reception area generally dingy and suspicious. Best avoided.

A huge building you can't miss is the **Suba Guest House** (tel. 2021845) near Regal Cinema in Colaba, which only has double rooms with common baths for Rs 199 (£7.95) per day. This hotel has over 50 rooms and there's a good chance of finding a place here.

Food

Bombay offers a vast choice of different kinds of cuisine and different ways of eating — from the ever-popular Frankies (Indianised frankfurters) which you get all over Bombay, to the new restaurant **Sheetal** in the suburb of Khar, which offers fresh seafood. There are tanks full of live fish, prawns and various types of crabs. Customers pick what they fancy and it's cooked for them just as they want it.

In the Colaba/Fort area are plenty of reasonably priced eating places like the **Yankee Doodle** fast food, **Edward VIII Restaurant, Woodside Inn,** the **Leopold Restaurant, Kailash Parbat Restaurant,** etc. Adjacent to the YWCA is the **Golden Gate Restaurant,** where you can have a very good salad lunch for Rs 35 (£1.40). **Woodside Inn** opposite the Regal Cinema offers a variety of *dosas* and pizzas. Try the unusual dry fruit pizza for Rs 20 (£0.80). Adjacent to Woodside Inn is the **Chickita Snack Bar,** good for a quick bite. The **Delhi Durbar Restaurant** in Colaba is a good place for reasonably priced Mughlai food. The **Leopold,** too, is a popular place although lately it has been having labour problems and the staff periodically go on strike. A little ahead of Leopold is **Food Inn,** with air-conditioned as well as non-air-conditioned dining halls. Food Inn has an Indian as well as a Chinese menu. The service is fast and the atmosphere very friendly.

In the Fort area, **Samovar,** the restaurant at the Jehangir Art Gallery, is definitely worth a visit. It is, in fact, a covered corridor converted into a restaurant which is always full. Here you'll rub shoulders with artists, students, the younger film stars and an assortment of interesting people. You can get chilled beer here at Rs 16 a bottle. There's a special fixed lunch menu every day at Samovar.

Behind Regal Cinema, toward the Gateway of India, are a row of Chinese restaurants such as the **Mandarin, Hong Kong** and **Nanking.** The food is uniformly good in all of them, Nanking being the most popularly frequented.

Churchgate, not too far from Colaba, also has a row of restaurants — **Gaylords, Talk of the Town, Berry's, Purohits Vegetarian Restaurant,** etc. And while in the Churchgate area don't miss **Rustom's** ice cream shop. His ice cream sandwiches are the best in Bombay.

If you want to eat in style, try the **Supper Club,** the rooftop night club at Hotel Oberoi Towers at Nariman Point. From here you get a fantastic view of the floodlit curve of Marine Drive,

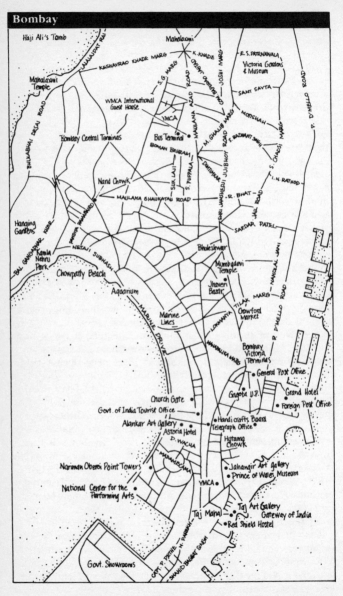

Bombay

popularly referred to as the Queen's Necklace. The Supper Club
has a dance floor with a good band and a continental menu. A
meal here costs anything upward of Rs 100 (£4) per head.

Hotel Ambassador at Churchgate has a revolving restaurant known as **The Top,** an unusual experience and a good place to eat. The **Shamiana** at Hotel Taj Mahal is a very popular 24-hour coffee shop, and if you know anyone at all in Bombay you'll bump into them here sometime or other.

The list of eating places in Bombay is endless. Best of all, beer is served in many restaurants at quite reasonable rates since Bombay has a very sensible policy regarding alcohol.

Sightseeing Highlights
▲▲▲A half-day City Sightseeing Tour is conducted by the MTDC. With limited time in a big city like Bombay, it is recommended that you join this trip, which includes:

Prince of Wales Museum — Built in 1914, this museum in the Fort area is named after King George V who, as Prince of Wales, laid the foundation stone in 1905. The museum has three main sections: Art, Archaeology and Natural History. The collections in each section are extensive. Here you can see a miniature model of the Parsis' Tower of Silence (The Parsis are a tiny but talented Indian community — Zubin Mehta, conductor of the New York Philharmonic, is one — who believe in leaving their dead in towers where they are eaten by vultures. Sounds gruesome, but the objective is to be of use to some living creature even in death.) The museum is closed on Mondays.

Gateway of India — This 26-metre-high stone archway facing the Taj Mahal Hotel was built to commemorate the visit to Bombay of King George V and Queen Mary in December 1911. The archway, declared open in December 1924 by the Viceroy of India, is also known as the Apollo Pier. The Elephanta Caves excursion starts from here. The Gateway of India is a popular place with tourists as well as locals, who can be seen here on family outings. The place is full of peanut sellers, pimps, smugglers hawking dubious goods and placid families. All coexist amiably.

Mani Bhavan — Mahatma Gandhi lived here from time to time between 1917 and 1934. It is known as Gandhi Memorial now, with a picture gallery and an impressive library of books by and on Mahatma Gandhi.

Hanging Gardens — A terrace garden built in 1880, it is called the Hanging Gardens because it is built on top of the water reservoir. The greenery around is a refreshing break from the unending concrete of Bombay.

Kamla Nehru Park — Named after Jawaharlal Nehru's wife, this garden, beautifully situated on the slopes of Malabar Hills, commands a panoramic view of Marine Drive and Chowpatty Beach. Definitely worth a visit just for the view.

World Dairy — The tour includes it for some unfathomable reason. Otherwise this is just a dairy for pasteurising, bottling and distributing milk.

Nehru Science Centre — A part of the half-day itinerary, the Centre has a museum, a children's science park and a permanent science exhibition. Closed on Mondays.

Taraporewala Aquarium — Built in 1951, the aquarium has interesting specimens of marine life. A pipeline brings water directly from the sea which is just across the road. Also on display are shells, shellcraft articles and fishery byproducts. An interesting place.

▲▲**Elephanta Caves** — An excursion to the Elephanta Caves needs three to four hours. The island of Elephanta is about 10 km northeast of Apollo Bunder. A harbour ferry service, with or without a guide, is run to the island by the State Tourism Department from the Gateway of India every hour from 0900 to 1400 hrs.

There are four rock-cut temples on the island, dating back to 450 to 750 AD. Named earlier as Gharapuri, in 1534 the island came under the Portuguese who named it Elephanta after the then existent rock-cut elephant near the landing place.

The caves in the island represent some of the best specimens of Brahmanical art and are connected with the worship of Shiva. There are some extremely fine pieces of sculpture here, each piece depicting a story connected with Lord Shiva. If you are an art lover, don't miss the Elephanta Caves.

TOURS 16 & 17

AURANGABAD

The original name for Aurangabad was Khidki, meaning 'window'. The city is indeed a window to a great cultural heritage. Though Aurangabad does have some attractions of its own, it is primarily a convenient base for visiting the magnificent cave temples of Ajanta and Ellora, which date back to 200 B.C.

Suggested Schedule

Tour 16

06:15	Depart Bombay for Aurangabad.
06:55	Arrive at Aurangabad Airport.
07:30	Travel to city, check into hotel.
09:30	Join all-day conducted tour to Ellora Caves and city sightseeing arranged daily by Maharashtra Tourism Development Corporation (MTDC, tel. 4713).
Evening	Visit Gulmandi, City Chowk and other shopping areas of Aurangabad.

Tour 17

08:00	Join the MTDC one-day excursion to the Ajanta Caves, 150 km away.
Evening	Relax.

Aurangabad

Aurangabad was declared in 1987 to have been the fastest growing city in Asia for three consecutive years. Its population has almost doubled during the last couple of years and is now about a million. Languages commonly spoken in Aurangabad are Marathi, Urdu and Hindi.

The best time to visit Aurangabad is from July to March, though the tourist traffic continues unabated throughout the year.

Moving around within the city is quite simple as distances are not exactly vast. The **Maharashtra Tourism Development Corporation** office (tel. 4713) is located in south Aurangabad near the railway station in a complex known as the **Holiday Resort**. MTDC conducted sightseeing excursion tours start and finish at the Holiday Resort, which also has accommodation facilities for tourists. There are also a number of restaurants and lodging houses in Station Road near the Holiday Resort. The government emporium and the post office are just across the road from the MTDC complex.

Station Road is a busy area, its most notable feature being the
large number of barbers who operate from the roadside, doing
brisk business. If you'll let them, they'll shave you exactly the
way your great-grandfather shaved, complete with leather strap for
the razor. They have a side business of cleaning out ears, and to
see them poke long, thin, lethal-looking metal spikes into
somebody's ear is to imagine that you've come upon a medieval
torture scene.

About five minutes' walk from the MTDC office is the
Government of India Tourist Office (tel. 4817), again in
Station Road. Mr Yadav, the Tourist Officer here, has loads of
information about the city and is most generous in imparting it.

The area immediately around the railway station is known as
the Paithan Gate area. The **Indian Airlines** city office (tel. 4864)
is in Adalat Road, about 15 minutes' walk from the railway
station. The city-airport coach service starts and terminates here.
Adjacent to the airline office is **Hotel Aurangabad Ashok** (tel.
4520), a Government of India enterprise. Between the station and
the airlines office is the **Youth Hostel** in the Padampura area.
The central bus station (tel. 4804) is nearby.

The northern part of the city comprises the busy market areas
such as Kranti Chowk, Gulmandi and City Chowk. Gulmandi
literally means 'flower market', and in the evenings it's just
that—with jasmine garlands sold at every corner. The narrow
streets of the shopping areas are an interesting place to walk.
Rubbing shoulders with you will be *burqua*-clad women, covered
from head to toe in shapeless black tents with a lace grill to peek
through, while other women zip past you on motorcycles.
Aurangabad, like India, is in rapid transition, and you'll get used
to such incongruous sights.

The **Himroo Weavers Co-operative Society** is in
Nawabpura, close to these shopping areas. Aurangabad has a
special handicraft known as *himroo*, handloom cotton and silk
interwoven with distinctive brocade designs. These can be used as
shawls, dresses, table and bed linen. Himroo designs have a
cotton warp and a silk weft and the literal meaning of the word
himroo is 'look-alike'. It looks like silk, while it's actually part
cotton. This craft was brought here by the Mughals. The
handloom himroo is more expensive than the mill-made one. The
Aurangabad Himroo Factory (tel. 3640) at Nawabpura has a
sales counter as well as traditional handloom weaving on display.

The airport lies to the east of the city, whereas the western part
comprises the Cantonment area. These are relics of the British
Raj where army units are still based.

Transport

Connected by air to Delhi and Bombay, Aurangabad Airport is 10

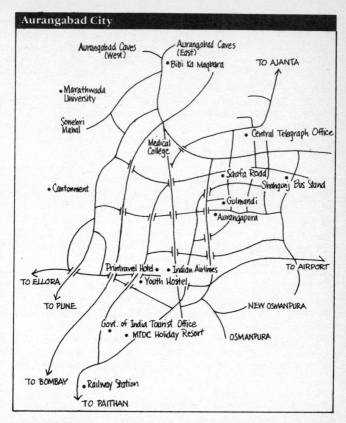

Aurangabad City

- Aurangabad Caves (West)
- Aurangabad Caves (East)
- Bibi Ka Maqbara
- TO AJANTA
- Marathwada University
- Sonehri Mahal
- Central Telegraph Office
- Medical College
- Sarafa Road
- Shahgunj Bus Stand
- Cantonment
- Gulmandi
- Aurangapura
- Printravel Hotel
- Indian Airlines
- TO AIRPORT
- TO ELLORA
- Youth Hostel
- TO PUNE
- NEW OSMANPURA
- Govt. of India Tourist Office
- MTDC Holiday Resort
- OSMANPURA
- TO BOMBAY
- Railway Station
- TO PAITHAN

km away from the city. There is a small information counter at
the airport. Indian Airlines operates a coach service to the city,
fare Rs 15 (£0.60). An auto rickshaw to the city charges a fixed
fare of Rs 25 (£1) and a taxi Rs 50 (£2). The drive from the
airport to the city is through an industrial zone, hardly the best
introduction to the legendary caves.

Metered auto rickshaws are a convenient way of moving
around. The cost from MTDC to Gulmandi will be about Rs 5.
(£0.20). The charge is Rs 2 for the first 1.6 km and Rs 1 for
every subsequent km. The few yellow-top taxis which operate in
the city charge Rs 2.30 for the first 1.6 km and Rs 1.50 for every
subsequent km. The city bus service operates from the railway
station to all the major points in the city.

If you're adventurous, *tongas* are a good way of moving around
and observing the city. *Tongas* are horse-drawn carriages
invariably combining a decrepit nag with an ill-tempered driver

who clears the path in front by abusing everything in sight. As you sedately clip-clop through the streets, you can pretend you're Ben Hur. Fares are negotiable but more or less the same as auto rickshaw fares.

Sightseeing Highlights

▲▲▲**Ajanta Caves**—Of all the ancient monuments in India, the murals of the rock-cut caves at Ajanta are special for their visual appeal and technical excellence. The caves are excavated in the semi-circular scarp of a steep rock about 76 metres high, overlooking a narrow gorge through which flows the stream Waghora. The caves, including the unfinished ones, are thirty in number; five are sanctuaries and the rest monasteries. They resolve themselves into distinct phases of Buddhist rock-cut architecture, spread over hundreds of years from the 2nd century BC to the 7th century AD. With the decay of Buddhism, the Ajanta caves went into oblivion and were rediscovered only in the year 1819, when a British hunting party happened to find them by sheer chance. Today these caves are part of the world's art heritage.

Within the framework of spirituality, an entire pageant of contemporary life has been vividly depicted in the paintings on the walls, while those on the ceilings are mainly decorative patterns. The paints were made from vegetation and pebbles of different colours found on the hillside. All the caves are numbered. Paintings in Caves 9 and 10 date back to the 2nd century BC. Among the best preserved caves are numbers 1, 2, 9, 10, 16, 17, 19, 21 and 26. As the interiors are very dark you should hire a portable light (Rs 5).

The murals are highly stylised but beautiful. The muted colours, the vivid rendering, the expressions, all are brought to the fore. Of the Ajanta beauties, the 'dark princess' with her soft, sensual appeal is the most famous. Before visiting Ajanta, try to buy D. Mitra's guide published by the Director-General, Archaelogical Survey of India (Price Rs 4) and available in any Aurangabad bookshop. The book explains each cave chronologically and contains much useful information. If you are keen on taking pictures, use fast films and take your tripod along. Flash photography is prohibited inside the caves.

Across from the Ajanta Caves is View Point, commanding a panoramic view of all thirty caves in the horseshoe-shaped ravine.

MTDC runs daily deluxe coach services to Ajanta at 08:00 to 18:00 hrs. The return fare is Rs 65 (£2.60). Ashok Travels and Tours (tel. 4143) run excursions to Ajanta by luxury bus for Rs 60 (£2.40) at 08:00 hrs. There are ordinary buses to Ajanta too, return fare Rs 39 (£1.55).

The caves are open daily from 09:00 to 17:30, Entry Rs. 50.

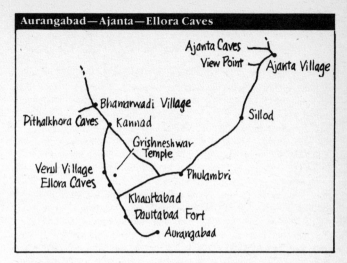

Aurangabad—Ajanta—Ellora Caves

▲▲▲**Ellora Caves**—30 km away from Aurangabad are the renowned rock-cut caves of Ellora, dating back to 600 AD. Unlike Ajanta, where all the caves are Buddhist, Ellora has 34 caves influenced by three religions: Buddhist, Hindu and Jain. There are no wall paintings, but the Ellora caves are famous for their wonderful sculpture. All the caves are numbered. Among the Buddhist caves, numbers 5, 10, 11 and 12 are regarded as the best examples; in the Hindu group, numbers 16, 21 and 29 are outstanding as having the best sculptures. Cave 16 (Kailash Temple) is perhaps the biggest monolith in the world. In the Jain group, Caves 32 and 34 have the best sculptures. The caves can be seen by daylight and you don't need a portable light.

MTDC runs a conducted luxury bus to the Ellora Caves at 09:30 to 18:00 hrs, Rs 50 (£2). An ordinary bus return to Ellora and the city, starting from the railway station bus stand, costs Rs 17 (£0.70). Ashok Travels and Tours do the same trip in a luxury bus for Rs 45 (£1.80). Besides Ellora, the City Tour includes visits to the Daulatabad Fort, the Grishneshwar Temple, Aurangzeb's Tomb, Bibi-ka-Maqbara and Panchakki.

The caves are open from 09:00 to 17:30 hrs, Entry Rs .50.

Daulatabad Fort—About 15 km from Aurangabad, en route to Ellora, rises the hilltop fortress of Daulatabad. In 1187, the fortress was built as the capital of the Hindu kingdoms in the Deccan. It was then known as Deogiri, the Hill of the Gods. The name Daulatabad, City of Fortune, was given by Muhammad Tughlaq in the 14th century when he shifted his capital here from Delhi. He is known as the Mad King because, after making the entire population of Delhi move out with him and travel 700 miles, tramping through forests and fighting off wild animals, losing hundreds of lives in the process, after a few months our hero tired of his new capital and led his remarkably meek subjects back to Delhi.

The outer wall of the fort runs for 6 km and there are several inner walls with heavy iron gates. Among the fort's remarkable features are the scarp, a deep moat and a spiral passage all hewn out of solid rock. Also worthy of attention is the Chand Minar, a striking tower. Entry to the fort is free.

In the shops at the entrance to the fort you'll see coins for sale dating back to the 14th-15th centuries. Even today these coins are excavated by the locals and sold for a song (but no antiques can be exported).

Grishneshwar Temple—Very near the Ellora Caves, this temple is one of the twelve sacred Jyotirlinga shrines (main shrines for the worship of Shiva), a place of pilgrimage for Hindus. A big religious fair is held here every March, on a date decided by the lunar calendar, and is open to the public. Entry to the temple is free.

Bibi-ka-Maqbara—5 km from Aurangabad, the mausoleum of Aurangzeb's wife is considered the finest Mughal monument in the Deccan. Built between 1657 and 1661, it is said to have been modelled on the Taj Mahal. Open sunrise to 20:00 hrs, entry Rs .50.

Panchakki—Another place on the city tour itinerary, Panchakki is actually within the city area. Dating back to the 17th century AD, water was harnessed to turn large grinding stones to mill flour. Open sunrise to 20:00 hrs, Entry Rs .50.

The tomb of a Muslim saint, Baba Shah Musafir, is also within this complex.

Accommodation

Hotel Rama International (tel. 8241) and **Hotel Ajanta Ambassador** (tel. 8211), both five-star hotels, are on the airport road.

The MTDC offers excellent accommodation at the **Holiday Resort**, a sprawling complex where singles cost Rs 45 (£1.80) and doubles Rs 80 (£3.20), all with attached baths. Check-out time is 08:00 hrs. **Tourist Home** (tel. 4212), a privately owned establishment adjacent to the Government of India Tourist Office, has doubles at Rs 40 (£1.60) upwards. Rooms are small but adequate. The lawns of the Tourist Home are a popular setting for marriages and wedding receptions. As you will doubtless discover, Indian marriages are colourful and exotic; they are also loud.

The **Youth Hostel** (tel. 3801) is a very pleasant place to stay, and offers dormitory accommodation at Rs 10 (£0.40) per bed.

But the gates of the youth hostel are locked every night at 22:00 hrs. The Warden, Lt. Col. Modak, is a stickler for discipline. (Not that Aurangabad has anything resembling nightlife).

Close to the Youth Hostel is **Hotel Panchavati** (tel. 5204) with singles for Rs 60 (£2.40) and doubles for Rs 70 (£2.80). It is a clean place, with a vegetarian restaurant attached. The **Printravel Hotel** (tel. 4707) in Station Road, under the able supervision of Mr. Printer, has singles at Rs 50 (£2) and doubles at Rs 90 (£3.60) upwards. The Foodwala's Bhoj Restaurant attached to this hotel is one of the best eating places in Aurangabad. The MTDC excursion coaches, which start from the Holiday Resort, also have a pick-up stop at this hotel.

Hotel Nandanvan (tel. 3311), also in Station Road, has singles for Rs 70 (£2.80) and doubles for Rs 100 (£4). Two popular restaurants, Rathi and Radhika, are part of this hotel complex.

Hotel Oberoi (not part of the luxury chain), tel. 3841, is in Osmanpura, an extension of Station Road. Singles are Rs 50 (£2) and doubles Rs 80 (£3.20) with attached baths. Haveli, a Chinese restaurant, is adjacent to this hotel.

In Station Road, closer to the railway station side, are a number of smaller hotels with tariffs ranging from Rs 30 to Rs 60 (£1.20-£2.40), such as **Hotel Guru** (tel. 4002), **Hotel Ashoka** (tel. 4555) and **Gitanjali Guest House** (tel 4674). These hotels offer cheap, very basic accommodation.

Food

Aurangabad does not have a distinct cuisine of its own, and most restaurants serve a variety of Indian food. The **Foodwala's Bhoj** vegetarian restaurant is reasonably priced and an excellent place to try a meal. The *thali* is a good buy at Rs 16 (£0.65). Try some local Marathi sweets here, like *basundi* (Rs 5) or *srikhand* (Rs 7). Both are milk-based and typically Maharashtrian, though sickeningly sweet. You can also try the Malai Makhan Kulfi (Rs 9), an ice cream served in a clay pot in which the milk is set.

The **Radhika Vegetarian Restaurant** (in Aurangabad you'll find a plethora of vegetarian restaurants) at Hotel Nandanvan is a very popular eating place and always packed at meal times. It offers South Indian, as well as other varieties of Indian food. The prices are very reasonable and the service is super-fast. Try the Hinty Minty ice cream (Rs 6). On a hot day it's the most refreshing dessert and the poetic name soothes as well.

The MTDC Holiday Resort has a restaurant called **Kailash** which serves a *thali* for Rs 9 (£0.35). Otherwise the menu is very limited.

Across from MTDC are a string of restaurants like **Guru, Shere-e-Punjab** and **Pinky**. The **Haveli** near Hotel Oberoi and **Mingling** on the airport road serve good Chinese food. **Diwan-e-**

Aam at Hotel Ajanta Ambassador has good Continental food, though it's quite expensive and quite far from the city.

Throughout the city are kiosks selling bottled milk called Energee at Rs 2.50 per bottle. It comes in four flavours and is bottled most hygienically at the Aarey Milk Plant near Bombay. It's quite safe and delicious.

Kashmir option

If you are taking this option you will need to curtail your stay in Aurangabad in order to return to Delhi (departure 07:25, arrival in Delhi 11:35). Use the time in Delhi to shop and catch up on any sightseeing you have missed, and remember to check your homeward flight.

TOUR 18

UDAIPUR

In Tour 3 you visited Jaipur in colourful Rajasthan. Now you're back in the desert state once again, this time in Udaipur, the city of lakes and palaces. Amidst the craggy Aravali Hills, Udaipur has some of the largest palaces in Rajasthan, lakes that are enchanting when they're full, spacious gardens and many historic monuments. The rugged sand dunes of Rajasthan recede into the background.

Suggested Schedule	
07:25	Depart from Aurangabad.
08:30	Arrive at Udaipur Airport.
10:00	Reach the city and check into a hotel. Freshen up for a busy and interesting day ahead.
11:00	Explore the city's sights and sounds on your own. It's easy to move around here with the help of a map.
13:00	Lunch.
14:00	City sightseeing.
Evening	On Wednesday and Saturday a folk cultural evening is arranged by the Rajasthan Tourist Development Corporation (RTDC) at one of the government-owned hotels. Entry is free. Otherwise, try boating on Fateh Sagar Lake. The area around the lake is illuminated in the evenings.

Udaipur

As your flight touches down at the little airport, you quickly forget you are in desert country. What you actually encounter is a lovely lake city with a population of about 300,000. Udaipur, in southern Rajasthan, is 577 metres above sea level. The climate is moderate (by desert standards, of course) throughout the year, though the best time to visit is between October and March.

The city was the location for the filming of the James Bond film *Octopussy,* a fact which makes the citizens inordinately proud. If you happen to be a critic of James Bond films and the simplistic warmongering they denote, Udaipur is not the best place to promote your views. The martial tradition remains strong here, and Mr. Bond is something of a local deity.

The old city, bounded by the remains of a 10-km-long city wall, is spread out on the eastern side of Lake Pichola. The city wall has eleven gates, Suraj Pol being the main entry gate.

The government emporium, Rajasthali, at Chetak Circle has a stock of interesting crafts. Take a leisurely 20-minute *tonga* ride from Chetak Circle to Hathi Pol, Delhi Gate and Suraj Pol (Rs 5) for a chance to relax and observe the busy streets.

Languages commonly spoken in the city are Rajasthani, Hindi, and of course English.

Transport

The Dabok Airport is 24 km from the city. For a tourist the only way to reach the city is to hire a private taxi, as there is no coach service, nor are auto rickshaws allowed inside the airport area. A taxi charges a fixed rate of Rs 75 (£3) to the city. Try to share it with fellow passengers. The officer at the Rajasthan Tourism counter at the airport can help you find a pool taxi, a vehicle that waits until it gets about five passengers. (More ambitious taxi drivers may well try to fit in fifty). After your early morning start, you may feel like snoozing off during the drive from the airport to the city. Don't, because on the way you can appreciate the countryside of this part of Rajasthan, with its abundant growth of cacti and generous sprinkling of ruins and old forts.

For moving around the city, unmetered auto rickshaws and *tongas* are easily available. Fares must be fixed in advance. Generally Rs 5 to Rs 10 can get you from any one point to another. There is a city bus service, but it is crowded and complicated. Avoid it. The best way to observe the city is to sit in a *tonga* and watch the world go by. A *tonga* ride from Chetak Circle to Hathi Pol, then on to Delhi Gate and Suraj Pol, costs about Rs 5. Private taxis can be hired in the city for about Rs 2 per km. The adventurous can hire a cycle from any cycle shop at 50 paise per hour or Rs 5 for the day.

Sightseeing Highlights

▲▲▲**Pichola Lake** — Maharana Udai Singh, the founder of Udaipur, was the scion of a clan that traces descent from Rama, the hero of the epic Ramayana, who is said to have been entranced by this lake. According to legend, Udai Singh came across the lake while hunting. Noticing a *sadhu* (mendicant), he sought his blessings and was told that if he built his capital here, it would never be captured. And so Udaipur came to be.

Now surrounded by hills, palaces, temples, bathing ghats and embankments, the Pichola Lake is the crowning glory of Udaipur. Set splendidly in the lake are two island palaces, the **Jag Mandir** and the **Jag Niwas.** For Rs 20 (£0.80) you can take a motor launch cruise to Jag Niwas, which is now Hotel Lake Palace. You

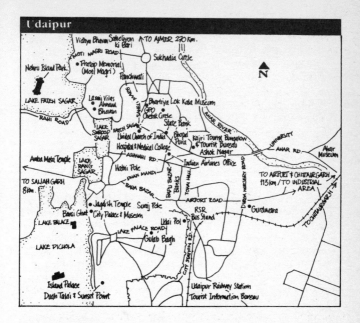

really must see this palace, with its cool marble interiors, liveried waiters and old world furniture.

City Palace and Museum — On the eastern side of Lake Pichola is the magnificent City Palace, with its own unique character. Made of granite and marble, the sparkling white filigreed balconies and windows, ornate arches and cupolas atop the towers add to the aura of magnificence. Construction of the palace was started by Maharana Udai Singh with the later Maharanas making additions. The main entrance to the museum is through Tripola, the triple gate. Eight exquisitely carved marble arches welcome the visitor. Inside the palace are the Sun Balcony, the Garden Palace. The Sheesh Mahal, Bhim Vilas, the Chini Chitrashala with its ornamented tiles, the Moti Mahal with delicate mirror work, and the Peacock Courtyard with lovely mosaics of peacocks, India's national bird. From inside the palace you can get an absolutely fantastic view of the Lake Palace Hotel shimmering like a white boat on the blue waters. Entrance fee to the City Palace Museum is Rs 3, open from 09:30 to 16:30 hours. You'll need about an hour to go around. Guides are available.

Lake Fateh Sagar and Pratap Memorial — This charming lake is surrounded on three sides by hills. On the Pearl hillock on the fourth side is the Pratap Memorial. In the midst of the lake, on an island, is Nehru Park, and for Rs 2 you can take a boat trip to the park. Boating hours are 08:00 to 20:00 hrs.

Pratap Memorial was erected in memory of Maharana Pratap, a monarch who defied the mighty Mughuls and who was described as 'the richest and most powerful monarch on this earth'. Known for his valour, the Maharana won back most of his strongholds from the Mughuls. The memorial overlooks Fateh Sagar Lake and commands a bird's eye view of Udaipur. You can pose in front of a bronze statue of Maharana Pratap on his horse, Chetak. Costumes are available for hire, in case you want to dress up for the photograph. Entry is Rs 1, open 09:00 to 18:00 hrs.

Saheliyon-ki-Bari (Garden of the Maids of Honour) — This garden, constructed by Maharana Sangram Singh in the 18th century, reveals the unique lifestyle of the royal ladies of Udaipur. It was designed for ladies who were sent by the Mughal Emperor as a peace offering to the Maharana. The spectacular garden has four pools, with ornate, delicately carved and chiselled kiosks and elephants in marble. There are fountains all along which will be switched on for you upon payment of Rs 2. There are a lotus pool, a marble throne and a beautiful garden to walk along. Entry to the gardens is Rs 1.50, open 09:00 to 18:00 hrs.

Bhartiya Lok Kala Museum — A small but interesting government-owned folk art museum with a rich collection of folk dresses, jewellery, musical instruments, folk deities, and paintings. A puppet show is performed for visitors free of charge. There is a display of intricate henna designs in the museum. Entry fee is Rs 1, open 09:00 to 18:00 hrs.

Jagdish Temple — Built in 1651 AD by Maharana Jagat Singh I, this temple is very near the City Palace. The largest temple in Udaipur, it enshrines a black stone image of Vishnu as Jaganath, Lord of the Universe. A long stretch of steps leads up to the temple.

Ahar Museum — East of Udaipur, in the crumbling remains of the ancient city of Ahar, are the royal cenotaphs of the Maharanas. Many marvel at the beauty of these pieces of architecture.

The Toy Train — The first of its kind in Rajasthan, the Toy Train Aravali Express, in the Sajjan Niwas Gardens close to the City Palace, is a 2 km circular ride. It takes children as well as adults around the gardens, deer yard, aviary, lions' den and lotus pond. It's an unusual and comfortable way to see the gardens.

Accommodation

Some of the most gorgeous palaces of Udaipur have now been converted into five-star hotels, such as **Hotel Lake Palace** (tel. 23241/5) and the **Shiv Niwas Palace Hotel** (tel. 25551/3). Single room tariffs at these hotels are Rs 600 to Rs 900 (£24-£36) and doubles Rs 700 to Rs 900 (£28-£36). Suites, where even

bathrooms have an attached lounge, can go up to Rs 3000 (£120)
a day. Staying at either of these hotels is sheer luxury. Udaipur
offers a wide variety of comfortable accommodation at rates
varying from cheap to reasonable to exhorbitant. You can have
your pick. Hotels with tariffs ranging from Rs 80 to Rs 120
(£3.20-£4.80) single and Rs 100 to Rs 190 (£4-£7.60) double
include the government-owned **Kajri Tourist Bungalow** (tel.
23509), the **Hotel Anand Bhawan** (tel. 23256), **Hotel Lakend**
(tel. 23841) and the **Ankur Hotel** (tel. 25355).

For the very reasonably priced hotels, try the Shastri Circle area
near the Kajri Tourist Bungalow. Most of the hotels here serve
only vegetarian food, but the tariffs are very low and
accommodation is quite comfortable. The **Ashok Hotel** (tel.
23925) at Shastri Circle has clean and comfortable singles with
attached baths at Rs 18 to Rs 25 (£0.70-£1), and doubles between
Rs 35 and Rs 50 (£1.40-£2). The tariff for rooms with a common
bath is as low as Rs 15 (£0.60) single, Rs 25 (£1) double. The
hotel has a wide terrace commanding a panoramic view of the
city. There is running water in all the bathrooms and hot water is
provided on request. Adjacent to the Ashok Hotel is **Prince
Hotel** (tel. 24355), in operation for the last 19 years. Facilities
provided include a phone and showers in the more expensive
rooms and a TV in the common lounge. Room tariffs are more or
less the same as the Ashok Hotel. The management of Prince
Hotel also runs the Ankur Hotel. Another pleasant hotel in the
Shastri Circle is **Hotel Alka** (tel. 23611) which has been catering
to tourists for the last 26 years. The management also owns Hotel
Lakend. Singles at Hotel Alka range between Rs 35 and Rs 60
(£1.40-£2.40), double from Rs 60 to Rs 85 (£2.40-£3.40). All 55
rooms in this massive three-storey building have attached
bathrooms. Mr. Pratap Singh Bhandari, the owner, takes personal
care and interest and the place is very efficiently managed.

Move a little to the south, toward the Town Hall Road.
Opposite the Ashoka Cinema is the government-run guest house,
Devsthan Vishranti Grih (tel. 23396). The entrance through a
side street is rather unimpressive, but once inside you will
discover it is a huge two-storey structure offering good
accommodation at very low rates. Here you are likely to rub
shoulders with visiting politicians and government officers (so
keep your hand on your wallet — Indian politicians are like their
brethren everywhere). Singles cost Rs 15 (£0.60) and doubles Rs
25 (£1). The rooms are big and airy and have attached
baths.There are eight dormitories as well, at Rs 5 (£0.20) per bed.
You won't find a cheaper place anywhere in Udaipur. In the
dining hall you can get a vegetarian *thali* for only Rs 8 (about
£0.30). Mr. Lodha, the manager, is an extremely helpful and
pleasant young man. This place is recommended for the tourist

on a tight budget.

Other hotels with tariffs ranging from Rs 40 (£1.60) for singles and Rs 60 (£2.40) for doubles are **Kalpana Hotel** (tel. 7507) and **Ram Niwas Palace Hotel** (tel. 23891) whose owner, Mr. Bhatti, has an American accent. Others include the **Payal Hotel** (tel. 24150) and **Yatri Hotel** (tel. 26775). The Palace Road, leading to the City Palace, has a number of hotels in the same tariff range.

Food

If you're looking for typical Rajasthani food in Udaipur, you are likely to be disappointed. But yes, there are many places with an elaborate menu offering Indian, Chinese and Continental food. A meal at either **Lake Palace** or **Shiv Niwas Palace Hotel** will be anything upward of Rs 100 (£4). At Chetak Circle, opposite the GPO, are the **Kwality** and **Berry** restaurants. Avoid Kwality, a dingy place with blaring music and a rude staff. (Kwality is the name of a chain of restaurants serving excellent food in the main cities of India, but this one doesn't seem to be part of the group.) Berry's is a better restaurant, with good food and service. A large bowl of pineapple *raita* (yogurt) at Rs 7 is a cool and refreshing starter to a meal.

In Town Hall Road, **Parkview Restaurant** can be recommended for good Chinese food. It's reasonably priced, too. For local flavour, try the **Natraj Restaurant** in Bapu Bazaar, behind the Ashoka Cinema. You will get excellent vegetarian food in a clean environment. A *thali* — quite an elaborate one, with unlimited helpings of food — costs Rs 11 for adults and Rs 6 for children. The proprietor, Mr. Srimali, can often be seen serving the guests himself and chatting with them.

Near Chetak Circle, the Hathi Pol and Suraj Pol areas have a number of bakeries, ice cream parlours and juice centres. Outside Chetak Cinema, at the **Vanilla Ice Cream Parlour,** you can have a massive helping of ice cream for Rs 5 or something rightly called the King Cone. If you have a sweet tooth, try a famous local sweet called *dil jaani* available at the **Sheesh Mahal Sweet House** near Delhi Gate.

TOUR 19

JODHPUR

Jodhpur, the gateway to the Thar Desert, receives abundant sunshine, even for these parts, and is therefore called 'City of the Sun'. An important fact most guidebooks seem to have missed is that Jodhpur is also the ancestral home of yours truly, your most humble guide. It is the city my grandfather eagerly left, believing that though it's a wonderful place to visit you wouldn't, as the saying goes, want to live there.

Suggested Schedule

08:55	Depart from Udaipur's Dabok Airport.
09:25	Arrive at Jodhpur airport.
10:30	Check into hotel.
11:00	Go to the railway station to get a return ticket to Jaisalmer on the overnight train. This booking must be done at Jodhpur.
12:00	Move around to get a feel of the city. An auto rickshaw from the station to Sardar Bazaar near the Clock Tower area will cost about Rs 4. Stop somewhere for a bite.
14:00	Join the half-day sightseeing trip starting from the Tourist Bungalow, or sightsee independently.
19:00	Watch as the pace of the city slows down. Visit the Sojati Gate/Jalori Gate areas. Have dinner before you leave, as the overnight train does not have a dining car. (Indian Railways meals are often surprisingly good, but the same can't be said for food sold on railway platforms.)
21:00	Collect your bags and you're off to the station.
22:15	Overnight train for Jaisalmer.

Jodhpur

Jodhpur was earlier known as Marwar or Marudesh, literally the 'Land of Sand'. When you arrive here you'll immediately know why. Today it is the second largest city in Rajasthan, with a population of about 500,000.

The princely state of Jodhpur was merged with Rajasthan in 1949. An an altitude of 230 metres above sea level, Jodhpur has a dry climate throughout the year. The best season to visit is

September to March. The old city is encircled by a stone wall,
built about a century after the city was founded in 1495, nearly
10 km in length with eight gates facing different directions.
Within the city walls stands the imposing fort on a low range of
sandstone hills.

Much of Jodhpur's modern development is accredited to
Maharana Jaswant Singh II, a very progressive ruler (1873-1895)
and therefore a maverick, considering the general run of rulers.
The new city lies at the foot of the hills. The clear distinction
between the old and new cities is visible from the ramparts of the
fort. The Tourist Office, Jodhpur Railway Station and post office
are outside the old city. The Tourist Bungalow and the Indian
Airlines Office are in the High Court Road.

Sajati Gate and its surrounding areas form the main city centre.
The roads there are congested with every conceivable type of
transport and a never-ending stream of pedestrians. Languages
commonly spoken are Hindi, Rajasthani and English.

Transport

The Ratanada Airport is only 5 km away from the city. Indian
Airlines operates an airport/city coach service for Rs 15 (£0.60).
Private taxis (about Rs 30 (£1.20) and auto rickshaws (Rs 20)
(£0.80) are easily available at the airport. Both are unmetered and
open to bargaining.

Jodhpur has a reasonably good bus service, as well as a *tempo*
service, though both get very crowded during office hours. The
tempo is a sort of elongated auto rickshaw, though smaller than a
van. It wobbles precariously on three wheels but is quite safe. It
usually has a set route and starts off when it's full, dumping and
picking up passengers along the way. It looks a little like a very
large, loud beetle.

Half-day sightseeing trips (fare Rs 20 (£0.80) start from the
Tourist Bungalow. For independent sightseers, half-day auto
rickshaw hire runs about Rs 50 (£2).

Sightseeing Highlights

▲▲▲**Mehrangarh Fort** — This massive, lofty red sandstone
fort overlooks the city from the hillock known as Chidia Khoont
(Bird's Nest), and rises 121 metres above the surrounding plains.
The fort was built in the incredibly short time of 29 days, after
the foundations were laid on May 12, 1559. Additions were later
made by different rulers.

This formidable fort remained practically unconquered for most
of medieval history. It has seven gates; the two main entrances
are Fateh Pol and Jai Pol. Walk up the zigzag way through the
various gates leading to the main premises of the fort. Each gate
has a rich history behind it. The Loha Pol (Iron Gate) is

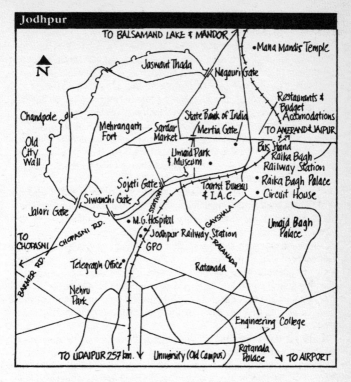

Jodhpur

TO BALSAMAND LAKE & MANDOR

• Maha Mandir Temple

Jaswant Thada

Nagauri Gate

Restaurants & Budget Accomodations

Chandpole

Mehrangarh Fort

Sardar Market

State Bank of India

Mertia Gate

TO AMER AND JAIPUR

Old City Wall

Bus Stand

Umaid Park & Museum •

Raika Bagh Railway Station

Sojati Gate

• Raika Bagh Palace

Tourist Bureau & I.A.C.

• Circuit House

Siwanchi Gate

Jalori Gate

• M.G. Hospital

Umaid Bagh Palace

TO CHOPASNI

CHOPASNI RD.

BARMER RD.

• Joodhpur Railway Station

GPO

Telegraph Office •

Ratanada

Nehru Park

Engineering College

TO UDAIPUR 257 km.

University (Old Campus)

Ratanada Palace

TO AIRPORT

considered very auspicious as it bears the *Sati ke thaape,* the imprint of hands of the 36 queens who ritually immolated themselves upon the pyres of their husbands. *Sati* was a particularly nasty Hindu ritual. It probably originated in women committing suicide to avoid rape, slavery or death after their husbands died in battle. Later it was broadened to include all women whose husbands died, even by natural causes. Much good *karma* was associated with a woman who committed *sati,* though whether the unfortunate victim regarded herself as being particularly blessed is not known.

Inside the fort are a series of courtyards and palaces. In the main courtyard is the Sringar Chowki (Coronation Throne), where the rulers of Jodhpur were crowned.

The palaces comprise a number of apartments. There is a *Palki* section with the royal palanquins on display. The elephant *howda* section displays gorgeous gold and silver *howdas.* (A *howda,* fixed onto an elephant's back, seats two or more and usually has a canopy.) There is a beautifully engraved silver *howda* of the Mughal Emperor Shah Jahan, who presented it along with an elephant and one hundred horses to Maharaja Jaswant Singh I in 1657 AD.

Other palaces include the Chandan Mahal (Sandalwood Palace), Deepak Mahal (Palace of Lamps) and the Jhanki Mahal (Palace of Glimpses) where women looked through slits in the wall at the world below, getting a glimpse *(jhanki)* but not being observed themselves. There is also the Moti Mahal (Pearl Palace) as well as a hall full of cradles used by royal infants over the years.

On the ramparts of the fort is an impressive collection of old cannons. You will be absorbed by the varied collection in the museum at the fort. From the fort, you can see the sprawling city of Jodhpur, with an array of houses painted blue which belong to members of the Brahmin community.

Entry fee — Rs 10; camera fee — Rs 10. Open 08:00-18:00 hrs. You'll need at least two hours to go around the fort.

▲▲▲**Umaid Bhavan Palace and Museum** — Founded by Maharaj Umaid Singh in 1929 on a 3.5-acre plot of land, the work on this palace was completed in 1942 by the continuous labour of 3,000 daily workers. Part of the palace is a hotel, while the other half is a museum. The royal family continues to live in the family suites on the hotel side. The museum has an interesting collection of old watches, books, hunting trophies and fine china and crystal ware. Entry fee — Rs 3. Open 09:00-17:00 hrs.

▲▲▲**Jaswant Thada** — Close to the fort, this is the royal crematorium built in 1899 in memory of Maharaja Jaswant Singh II. The cenotaphs house portraits of the rulers showing the genealogy of the dynasty. The portrait of Maharaja Jaswant Singh II is worshipped, and people come to pray that their wishes will be fulfilled. The building has translucent marbles fixed into the walls; light passes through them throughout the day. Entry is free. Open 08:00-18:00 hrs.

▲▲**Mandore Gardens** — Nine km away from Jodhpur city, this was the old capital of Marwar. Its ancient name was Mandaya Pura, and it has great historical as well as archaeological importance. Mandore was once the royal crematorium grounds, and cenotaphs of the rulers can be seen here. Most of the cenotaphs are built in the shape of Jain temples. The Mandore Gardens are today a popular picnic spot. There is a city bus service every half hour. Entry is free. Open all day.

▲**Maha Mandir Temple** — Two km away from the city, this temple is a place where sacred glory reigns in peaceful tranquillity. Situated in Mandore Road, the temple is an architectural marvel supported by one hundred pillars and ornamented with detailed designs and figures depicting various yoga postures.

▲**Government Museum** — Nestled in the middle of the Umaid

Public Garden, this museum has a rich collection of exhibits displaying armour, textiles, local arts and crafts, miniature paintings, old manuscripts and more. Entry fee is Rs .50, open 10:00 to 16:30 hrs.

Accommodation

This is not an overnight halt according to our itinerary, but here is some information on Jodhpur accommodation just in case.

Umaid Bhawan Palace Hotel (tel. 22366), often called 'the pink Taj Mahal', is Jodhpur's most luxurious hotel, with 62 palatial rooms and all facilities including a swimming pool and health club. Tariffs start at Rs 550 (£22) single and Rs 650 (£26) double. The hotel is worth a visit just to see its grandeur.

The **Ajit Bhawan Legendary Resorts** (tel. 20409) is another palace converted to a hotel. Despite its candidly grandiose name, it is quite good and has an ethnic air about it. There are cottage-type bungalows, done up in Rajasthani style, with spacious lawns. Tariff is Rs 250 (£10) for a single and Rs 350 (£14) for double occupancy. The buffet, a lavish spread of excellent Indian food, costs Rs 50 (£2). Maharaj Swaroop Singh, the owner and a relative of the present Maharaja, is generally around and service is very personal.

Near the airport, and therefore convenient, is the **Hotel Ratanada** (tel. 25911). Tariff is Rs 400 (£16) upwards.

Among reasonably priced places, the **Ghoomer Tourist Bungalow** (tel. 21900) has very good rooms at Rs 40 (£1.60) for singles with a common bath and Rs 80 (£3.20) with an attached bath. The service is very satisfactory, and the management is generally helpful. If you don't check in, you can still use their left luggage facilities. **Hotel Galaxy** (tel. 20796), a large building in Sajati Gate, has singles for Rs 35 (£1.40) and doubles for Rs 60 (£2.40), all with attached baths.

Near the Jodhpur railway station are a number of hotels for the budget tourist, though some of these don't give rooms to foreigners because of the official formalities like filling in various forms. (Jodhpur is very near the border with Pakistan, and much smuggling is carried on. Only the government of India could believe that filling in forms would catch or deter a genuine smuggler. But it does annoy the authentic tourist.) The **Shanti Bhawan Lodge** (tel. 21689) opposite the railway station offers rooms at Rs 30 (£1.20) for singles and Rs 55 (£2.20) for doubles. Foreigners are welcome here. The rooms are rather small, but comfortable. Some other cheap but good and clean places are the **Adarsh Niwas Hotel** (tel. 26936), the newly opened **Hotel Marudhar** (tel. 22736) and a string of hotels in the Sajati Gate area. Since you'll be travelling overnight by train, you could also try the **Railway Retiring Rooms** at the station (tel. 22741).

Your train ticket entitles you to use these facilities for a nominal payment.

Food

Jodhpur is a good place to try out local food and drink. The **Marwar Hall** at Hotel Umaid Bhawan serves excellent Rajasthani cuisine in royal style. The buffet is priced at Rs 60 (£2.40). At Jalori Gate, **Pankaj Restaurant** is renowned for its excellent vegetarian fare. Here for between Rs 30 and 40 (£1.20-£1.60) you get a good meal and can eat in quiet comfort. The **Kalinga Restaurant** (tel. 24068) opposite the railway station is generally crowded and very popular with tourists. It is a western style restaurant serving Indian, Continental and Chinese food. Again, Rs 30-40 (£1.20-£1.60) can get you a very good meal.

A number of restaurants and *bhojanalayas* near the station offer *thali* meals with vegetarian food served in local style. Prices range from Rs 8 to Rs 10 (£0.30-£0.40). The very reasonably priced **Coffee House** at Sahati Gate specializes in South Indian food.

As you walk down Station Road, look for **Samosa House** adjacent to the Minerva Cinema. It is a fairly clean snack bar with excellent service. Try the Makhani Lassi. *Lassi* is best described as buttermilk. It is made by adding water to yogurt and beating the mixture vigorously. *Lassi* comes sweetened or salted and is very refreshing drink. At Rs 3.50 you get a glass of *lassi* with chunks of fresh butter in it. You might also try the Sponge Rasmalai (Rs 4 per plate), another Jodhpur speciality. Dilip Singh, the manager at Samosa House, is a culinary expert and can enlighten you on a variety of Rajasthani sweets and snacks.

TOUR 20

JAISALMER

Often referred to as the 'City of Gold', Jaisalmer in the heart of the Thar Desert holds an exotic fascination for any traveller to India. The city is endowed with a rich historic and legendary past. It was once an important transit point on the prosperous camel trade route between India and central Asia. Today you can see caravans of camels still used by villagers, as well as by tourists on the ever-popular camel safaris.

Suggested Schedule

07:30	Arrive by overnight train at Jaisalmer station.
08:00	Optional: Check into hotel. (You are not scheduled to spend the night here but may want to deposit your baggage and freshen up before starting the day.)
09:00	Explore Jaisalmer, either with a half-day sightseeing tour or preferably, on your own. Walking through the streets at your own pace is the only way to really see the city.
12:00	Brunch.
13:00	Join a conducted jeep trip to Lodarva, visiting the Amar Sagar and Bada Bagh en route.
15:00	Just wander — you can't get lost in Jaisalmer. Shoppers will find exquisite silver jewellery and fine embroidered leather goods.
19:00	Return to hotel. Pack up and depart for the railway station to catch the overnight train leaving for Jodhpur at 2010 hrs.

Jaisalmer

Deep in the western Rajasthan desert, Jaisalmer is situated about 793 metres above sea level. The climate is generally dry and hot, and the best time to visit the city is between October and March. After March it gets unbearably hot and windy. The annual Desert Festival of folk dances, songs and a carnival is held in February.

Once a strategic military outpost, the city is surrounded by a 5 km long stone wall, supported by bastions and corner towers. There are two main entrances to the city — the Garsisar Gate leading from the east and the Amar Sagar Gate from the west.

The gates are strongly built of cut stone, cemented together with lime and arched overhead.

Within the city walls the fascinating streets of Jaisalmer bustle with people, shops and cows. Remember, all cows are holy. Indeed, nowhere else in India except perhaps at Varanasi will you see such a good example of peaceful coexistence between cows and man. Manak Chowk (the main market), inside the city and near the fort, is always bubbling with activity.

To get the feel and impact of Jaisalmer, watch the city from the terrace of any one of its magnificent mansions. Apart from the spectacular beauty, you'll find an amazing harmony between the city and the landscape. The houses, even newly constructed ones, are made of golden yellow sandstone, and the colours merge with the vast stretches of surrounding sand. It is a fascinating sight of shapes and forms in varying shades of gold.

Languages commonly spoken are Rajasthani and Hindi. Due to the heavy tourist inflow, many locals now speak English of a peculiar sort, and the children of Jaisalmer are likely to greet you with 'You coming which country?' Be friendly.

Transport
Jaisalmer was, until recently, connected to Delhi by air. Of late, however, the flights have been suspended indefinitely due to its proximity to India's sensitive border with Pakistan. Jaisalmer is connected by rail and road to Jodhpur (285 km), with daily service on the overnight train and a day train.

When you look at the map of Jaisalmer, you'll notice the railway station tucked in one corner on the west, apparently a long distance from the city. However, it isn't as remote as it seems, since the total area of Jaisalmer is a mere 5.1 square kilometres. The population is about 20,000 — with a large floating population of tourists, of course. At the Jaisalmer railway station, jeeps and auto rickshaws are available for transport to the city, a few minutes' drive. Hiring a jeep to the city costs Rs 10 (about £0.40), and an auto rickshaw about Rs 5. Taxis charge Rs 2 per km.

Auto rickshaws, freely available in the city, generally charge a fixed rate of Rs 4 from one point to another. Cycle rickshaws can be hired at Rs 1 per hour or Rs 6 for a day. But the best way to see the city is to walk around so you can stop and marvel at the beautifully filigreed and colourfully painted homes. For moving around within the city complex you really don't need a conveyance.

Sightseeing Highlights
▲▲▲The Fort — The second oldest in Rajasthan, the Jaisalmer Fort stands on Tricuta Hill 250 feet above the surrounding

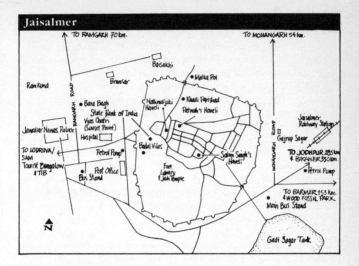

Jaisalmer

country. Built in 1156 AD by Maharawal Jaisal, the fort has four gates, with the massive Suraj Pol as the main entrance. One-fourth of the population of Jaisalmer lives within the walls of this fort.

It's an unforgettable experience to walk inside the citadel, which is full of ancient mansions and latticed balconies exuding an old world charm. The centuries slip away. Men in their colourful turbans and women in swirling skirts and chunky jewellery move around their homes within the fort, while children are busy playing cricket in the streets. Bringing you forcefully back to the present are the rows of TV antennae that dot the skyline. It's a charming fusion of ancient and modern.

Within the fort are the palaces — five beautifully carved Raj Mahals constructed at different times by different rulers. The palaces have exquisite paintings and delicately carved stone balconies from which you see a bird's eye view of the city.

▲▲▲**Jain Temples** — Within the fort walls are eight Jain temples, built between the 12th and 15th centuries, of which the Chintamani Parshvanath Temple is the oldest. Each temple has an elaborately carved *torana* or arch at the entrance. Shoes, cameras and leather items are not allowed inside the temple. These Jain temples have detailed and intricate carvings depicting scenes from Hindu mythology. There are some excellent carvings of birds and animals as well. The temple also houses a library, the Gyan Bhandar, established in 1500 AD. It has about three thousand ancient manuscripts, some of the oldest and rarest in India, on palm leaves and wood from pre-Mughal and Rajput times. Entry is free.

▲▲▲**The Havelis** — Jaisalmer's pride is its ancient *havelis* or
residential mansions, built by the city's wealthy merchants. Of
these, the three most popular are Salim Singh ki haveli,
Nathmalji ki haveli and Patwon ki haveli, which are now national
monuments. Entrance is free. Open 10:30 to 17:00 hrs.

Salim Singh was the Prime Minister of Jaisalmer about 200
years ago. His house, the magnificently carved Salim Singh ki
haveli, towers above the rest of the city. It is a grand six-storey
edifice of cut stones and much ornamentation, especially on the
top storey. There are 38 balconies carved in different designs,
each more attractive than the last. This unique mansion is
distinguished by its arched blue roof, supported by numerous
brackets carved in the form of peacocks. Part of the *haveli* is lived
in by the owners; the other part is rented out as office space.

Nathmalji ki haveli, built in the year 1885, was also once a
Prime Minister's residence. The carvings were done by two
Muslim brothers who were renowned stone carvers of Jaisalmer
state. The front edifice has delicately arched windows, while walls
in the interior are decorated with paintings in the miniature style.
Elephants carved out of yellow sandstone still guard this huge
five-storey edifice where Nathmalji's grandchildren continue to
live with their families.

Patwon ki haveli — the five beautiful apartments built by the
Patwa brothers from 1800 to 1860 AD — are the most spectacular
of all Jaisalmer's *havelis*. The ceiling of this five-storey wonder is
supported by handsomely carved and polished pillars. One storey
is richly adorned with painted murals.

▲▲▲**Gadi Sagar Tank** — Built by Maharawal Garai in 1367
AD, the tank lies south of the city walls. Once it supplied water
to the city but now it is more or less dry. Around the tank are
four Hindu temples with *chattris* (*chattri* means 'umbrella'),
ornately carved canopies. There is an arched gateway to the lake
and numerous gardens and shrines all around. In winter there is a
huge variety of bird life.

Lodarva/Amar Sagar — Seventeen km northwest of Jaisalmer
lies Lodarva, the ancient capital of Jaisalmer. There are numerous
Jain temples built in 1600 AD with ornate carved arches at the
entrance and a Kalpataru (divine tree) within its complex. On the
drive to Lodarva you will see flocks of peacocks.

Close to Lodarva is Amar Sagar, built in 1740 AD. It was once
a royal garden with a lake which has since dried up. Today Amar
Sagar is a small but busy village where restoration work is going
on to renovate an ancient Jain temple.

▲▲**Bada Bagh** — These are the royal cenotaphs built by
Maharana Jaita Singh in 1554 AD, six km away from Jaisalmer,
located amidst thickly grown trees and a stream. The carved
images of former rulers on horseback are imposing. There is a

huge dam adjacent to Bada Bagh.

Accommodation

To the west outside the city walls are the government-run **Moomal Tourist Bungalow** (tel. 92) and the **Jaisalmer Niwas Palace Hotel.** Don't even step into the latter. A palace turned into a hotel, the place is deplorably shabby and ridiculously expensive with single rooms at Rs 350 (£14). The food is awful and priced at an excessive Rs 70 (£2.80) per meal. The service, too, leaves a lot to be desired. The **Moomal Tourist Bungalow,** on the other hand, is an excellent place — pleasant, clean and comfortable. Rooms are available at Rs 40 (£1.60) upwards. But the food is also pretty bad.

ALTERNATIVE: TOURS 18, 19 & 20

SRINAGAR

If you are travelling between March 15 and October 15, we
suggest that on your last days in India you visit cool alpine
Kashmir instead of baking in the desert. A jewel in the heart of
the Kashmir Valley, Srinagar is often referred to as the
'Switzerland of the East'. Literally, *sri* means 'beauty' and *nagar*
stands for city, and this is truly the city of beauty. Srinagar is a
popular tourist destination, and a worthwhile addition to your
itinerary, at any time of year.

Suggested Schedule

Tour 18

10:15	Arrive from Delhi (IC 427).
15:00	Check into hotel or houseboat.
17:00	*Shikara* (small boat) ride on the Dal/Nagin Lakes. Sunset over the lake is spectacular.
Evening	Visit the city shopping areas which remain open until late in the evening. *Son-et-lumiere* show at Shalimar Bagh (tickets Rs 4 and Rs 10).

Tour 19

	One-day excursion into the beautiful countryside — Gulmarg or Pahalgam.

Tour 20

08:30	Half-day sightseeing in Srinagar.
13:30	Leave for airport.
15:15	Flight departure.

Srinagar

Capital of Jammu and Kashmir, the northernmost state of India,
Srinagar is situated in the lap of the Himalayas, at an altitude of
1560 metres, or 5200 feet, above sea level, on both banks of the
river Jhelum which is spanned by nine bridges. The eastern
suburbs of the city extend to the shore of the Dal Lake. Spring-
fed, the 6 km long, 3 km wide lake is divided into four distinct
parts by causeways — Gagribal, Lokutdal, Boddal and Nagin.
Moored along the banks of the lake are Srinagar's unique
houseboats — ornately carved, richly furnished, with exotic

names. Srinagar has a population of almost a million. Languages commonly spoken are Urdu and Hindi.

The road running along the Dal is known as the Boulevard. Various hotels and fashionable shopping centres are located here. About ten minutes' walk from the Boulevard is the Tourist Reception Centre (tel. 72698) which also houses the City Airlines office (tel. 73231) and the J & K State Government Information offices. This is also the bus terminus for city sightseeing as well as excursion tours around Srinagar. The coach service to the airport also starts from the TRC. The Government Arts Emporium (tel. 73012) is a further ten minutes' walk to the west of the TRC.

Parallel to the TRC is Maulana Azad Road, which leads to Residency Road, the modern commercial centre of Srinagar. Hotel Broadway and Hotel Nedous are located here. Srinagar's polo grounds also run along Maulana Azad Road. In Residency Road is the State Bank of India Foreign Exchange Department.

A 15-minute walk down Residency Road leads to Lal Chowk in old Srinagar. This is a very busy shopping centre where Kashmiri handicrafts, different qualities of saffron, carpets, etc. are available. A number of budget hotels are located here as well as in Wazir Bagh. An auto rickshaw from the TRC to Lal Chowk costs about Rs 5. Walking there will take a good half-hour.

Srinagar's All India Radio Building is just across the road from the TRC. Behind the AIR Building, across Zero Bridge, is the Raj Bagh area, where a number of guest houses have sprung up offering accommodation at very reasonable rates.

Rising behind the Boulevard and commanding a magnificent view of the Dal Lake is Shankaracharya Hill, where a temple draws a constant stream of visitors. The Srinagar TV tower is also atop this hill.

The Tourist Directory available from the TRC (Rs 7) gives useful tourist information as well as a map of Srinagar.

Transport

At a distance of 876 km from Delhi, Srinagar is well-connected with Delhi and Bombay by road as well as air. The nearest railhead is Jammu, 305 km away. Srinagar Airport is about 14 km from the city. There is a bus service (fare Rs 13 (£0.50)) from the airport to the centrally located Tourist Reception Centre (TRC). The Indian Airlines office is also in the TRC building. Taxi fare to the city is fixed at Rs 46 (£1.85). On the big board outside the airport building, taxi fares to various destinations are prominently displayed.

There is a Tourist Information counter at the airport. Hotel and houseboat bookings can be made at the airport.

The drive from the airport to the city is a beautiful prelude to

your sojourn in this valley, which is often described by poets as a
paradise on earth.

In the city, auto rickshaws are easily available. They have
meters, but generally charge a fixed fare. The city bus service is
confusing and infrequent. There is a point-to-point Matador van
service which is quite efficient (fare Rs .70). Tourist taxis are also
available (fare Rs 3.10 for the first 2 km, Rs .28 every subsequent
150 metres). The Tourist Taxi Stand (tel. 74898) is at Lal
Chowk, though taxis are available all over the city. In addition,
there are some yellow-topped, yellow stripped, metered taxis in
the city. Contact the Tourist Police, tel. 77303.

Shikaras (gondola-type boats) on the Dal and Nagin Lakes have
fixed fares which are prominently displayed on boards along the
banks. They generally charge Rs 20 for an hour's ride. Many
shikaras crisscross the water selling flowers, fruits and handicrafts.
Remember to carry some small change with you. Children will
invariably paddle up to your boat, offer you a flower and wait for
a tip. Rs .50 to Rs 1 is an expected tip for this gesture.

Shopping

The bazaars in Srinagar, full of colourful crafts, are spread along
the old as well as the new parts of the city. You can get a variety
of stone, the famed *Pashmina* and Kashmiri embroidered shawls
and *Phirans* (dresses), gorgeous carpets, carved walnut furniture,
papier mache articles, leathers and furs — the list is almost
endless. Even window-shopping is fun in Srinagar. The
Government Emporium has fixed rates, but the other shops are
open to bargaining. However, they are so used to haggling with
tourists that they drive a hard bargain.

The **Suffering Moses** is close to the Tao Garden Cafe (see
'Food'). Run by an elderly couple, this shop displays a variety of
Kashmiri handicrafts. Shopping here is a pleasure, though prices
are on the high side.

Srinagar Sightseeing Highlights

The State Tourism Department conducts half-day city sightseeing
tours for Rs 25 (£1), starting from and terminating at the TRC.
Sightseeing can also be done independently. Bicycles are available
for hire at Rs 10 per day from cycle shops at the boulevard.
Shikaras can also be engaged to visit the Mughal Gardens and the
Hazratbal Mosque.

▲▲▲**Shalimar Gardens** (14 km) were built by Emperor
Jehangir. Very well-maintained, they offer a pleasant place to
walk. An open-air *son-et-lumiere* (sound and light) show is offered
every evening. The show, in English, starts at 21:00 hrs and lasts
for about an hour. Tickets are Rs 4 and Rs 10. There are special
buses to the city at the end of the show. Auto rickshaws are also

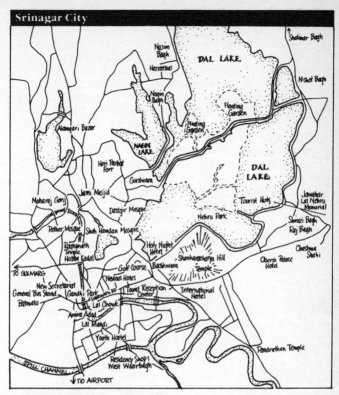

Srinagar City

available (Rs 20 (£0.80) one-way).

▲▲▲**Nishat Bagh** (11 km) is truly a 'garden of pleasure', beautifully located with the mountains as a backdrop. Built in the year 1633, this is the largest Mughal garden in Srinagar.

▲▲▲**Pari Mahal** — literally meaning 'palace of the fairies' — is about 10 km from the TRC. A favourite location for film shootings, it has a series of terraces and lovely rose gardens and is illuminated in the evenings.

▲▲▲**Chashma Shahi** (9 km) — the springs in this garden are said to have medicinal properties. The garden, on a split level, is a popular picnic spot. Lots of souvenir shops outside.

▲▲▲**Hazratbal Mosque** — A beautiful white building 7 km away, which can be spotted from a distance. It houses a relic — the hair, it is said, of the Prophet Muhammad, which is displayed on special occasions.

▲▲▲**Shankaracharya Hill** — Known earlier as Takht-i-Sulaiman, the hill has a temple on top. The road is motorable up to a point, after which 200 steps must be climbed to reach the temple. The hilltop provides a magnificent view of Srinagar city.

Sightseeing Excursions

We recommend a one-day excursion into the countryside. The
Tourism Department organises various trips. Two popular
destinations are Gulmarg and Pahalgam. The choice is yours.
One-day return coach trips to Pahalgam start from the TRC every
morning at 08:00 hrs. The coach for Gulmarg departs at 09:00
hrs for the one-day round trip. Fare for either trip is Rs 45
(£1.80).

The State Tourism Department also runs a helicopter service
every day over the city (Rs 200 (£8), to Gulmarg and back (Rs
200 (£8), and to Pahalgam and back (Rs 500 (£20)). Taking a
helicopter is not really the best way to see the countryside,
though it can save a lot of time. More information about the
helicopter service is available from the TRC.

Gulmarg, literally meaning 'meadow of flowers', is 56 km
northwest of Srinagar. A poplar-lined road runs from Srinagar for
38 km to a place called Tangmarg which commands a fabulous
view of the mountains. From here, the uphill drive starts as the
road passes through the majestic, pine-covered terrain to
Gulmarg.

The 3.5 km long, one km wide meadow of Gulmarg has a lot
to offer the tourist. Every season has its own delights. The
18-hole golf course at Gulmarg, laid according to international
specifications, is the world's highest, at an altitude of about 3,000
metres. There is a ropeway, or go on a pony ride, or simply walk
around the beautiful meadow.

You can get to Khilanmarg, a highland meadow about 4 km
from Gulmarg, on ponies or on foot. Khilanmarg offers a
panoramic view of the snow peaks and also the Wular Lake (the
largest freshwater lake in India) in the distance. Gulmarg is also a
popular winter resort, and from December onwards winter sports
enthusiasts come here in full force for skiing holidays.

Pahalgam, 96 km east of Srinagar and 2,400 metres above sea
level, has always been a favourite with tourists. The Lidder River
runs through Pahalgam's majestic setting. The state government
conducted excursion to Pahalgam halts at various interesting
places en route, like the famous gardens at Pampore, the centre of
Kashmir's saffron industry. You get a taste of history at
Avantipur, where you see the ruins of two Hindu temples built in
the 9th century AD. Another stop en route to Pahalgam is
Achabal, a garden built by the Mughals in the year 1620.

Apart from the scenic beauty, Pahalgam is a popular take-off
point for treks into the Himalayas. Walking in the Lidder Valley
through forests of pine, fording crystal-clear mountain streams
and strolling in beautiful meadows full of wild flowers, make for

truly memorable experiences.

Accommodation

Among the five-star hotels, there are the **Oberoi Palace** (tel. 75617), **Centaur Lake View** (tel. 75621) and **Broadway** (tel. 79001). **Nedou's** (tel. 73015), one of the oldest luxury hotels of Srinagar, is used frequently as a base to prepare for explorations into the Himalayas.

J & K State Tourism offers good accommodation in the city at very reasonable tariffs. The **Tourist Reception Centre** has singles at Rs 50 (£2) upwards and doubles at Rs 80 (£3.20). The other two government-owned hotels are **Lalla Rukh Hotel** (tel. 71078) and **Hotel Badshah** (tel. 76063), both close to each other in the Lal Chowk area. Tariffs in both are Rs 90 (£3.60) upwards for double rooms.

As for privately owned accommodation, Srinagar has a wide network of hotels and guest houses all over the city. In the Boulevard area, along the Dal Lake are hotels with tariffs from Rs 100 (£4) upwards. **Hotel Shahenshah Palace** (tel. 75856) has doubles from Rs 200 (£8) to suites for Rs 1100 (£44). The **Trambo Continental** (tel. 73914) has singles at Rs 200 (£8) and doubles at Rs 240 (£9.60). **Hotel Ornate, Nehru's, Hotel Zabarvan** (tel. 71442) and **Shah Abbas** (tel. 77789) are some other hotels with tariffs from Rs 150 (£6) upwards. **Hotel Madhuban** (tel. 72478), located in Nehru Park (one of the islands in the Dal Lake) has singles at Rs 70 (£2.80) and doubles at Rs 90 (£3.60). Along the Boulevard, near the Coins restaurant, is the **Basu Guest House,** a neat little place run by Dr. Basu with doubles for Rs 100 (£4).

For very inexpensive accommodation in the city, come to the Wazir Bagh area. The **Youth Hostel,** adjacent to the Stadium, has dormitory accommodation at Rs 5 (£0.20) per bed.

Opposite the Youth Hostel is **Hotel Ellora** (tel. 30528), efficiently run by the Madan brothers. It was a sprawling home, now converted into a hotel with large and airy rooms. Singles cost Rs 20 (£0.80) and doubles Rs 30 (£1.20), all with attached baths. There is a nice lounge/dining hall with a TV. Close to the Ellora is the **Habib Guest House** (tel. 31249) with singles at Rs 70 (£2.80) and doubles at Rs 120 (£4.80).

Hotel New River View, a deluxe hotel between Lal Chowk and Wazir Bagh, has singles at Rs 120 (£4.80) and doubles at Rs 150 (£6). The Cellar restaurant in this hotel serves Kashmiri cuisine.

Quite close to Wazir Bagh is Badshah Chowk, where **Hotel Jahangir** (tel. 71830) is an excellent hotel overlooking the secretariat buildings. Singles are Rs 110 (£4.40) and doubles Rs 195 (£7.80).

Across Zero Bridge, less than a kilometre away from the TRC, is the Raj Bagh area. **Zero Inn** (tel. 77904) offers singles at Rs 55 (£2.20) and doubles at Rs 75 (£3), all with attached bathrooms. The rooms are quite comfortable. A restaurant serves Indian, Continental and Chinese food. **Kohsheen Guest House** (tel. 72528) has singles at Rs 50 (£2) and doubles at Rs 70 (£2.80) with attached baths. A dormitory bed here costs Rs 15 (£0.60). **Happy Home, Soni** and (astonishingly) **King Pizza** are some other guest houses, all within walking distance of each other. Tariffs in all range from Rs 50 to Rs 100 (£2-£4).

There are a number of hotels close to the Dal and Nagin Lakes. **Hotel Mir Palace** (tel. 74877) has singles at Rs 70 (£2.80) and doubles at Rs 80 (£3.20), all with attached baths. **Hotel Lakeside** has singles for Rs 50 (£2) and doubles for Rs 70 (£2.80) with attached baths.

Houseboats: Moored on the banks of the river Jhelum, and in the Dal and Nagin lakes, houseboats have a fascinating aura of their own. A houseboat ranges from 24 to 36 metres in length, and is between three and six metres wide. Bedrooms have attached bathrooms with hot and cold running water, and the living rooms are generally well-furnished. There are decks for sunbathing. A small *shikara* boat is always around for quick trips across the lake.

The houseboats are classified, according to the facilities they offer, into Deluxe, A, B, C and D categories. The tariffs generally include board and lodging. Deluxe has singles at Rs 275 (£11), doubles at Rs 405 (£16.20). Category A has singles for Rs 170 (£6.80) and doubles at Rs 250 (£10). Category B has singles for Rs 120 (£4.80) and doubles at Rs 200 (£8). Category C has singles at Rs 80 (£3.20) and doubles at Rs 140 (£5.60). The Tourist Department has a list of approved houseboats, and you can make your bookings from the Houseboat Owners Association counter at the TRC. It's best that you go through them and don't try to hire a houseboat on your own. They'll overcharge you.

Food

Traditional Kashmiri cooking is of two types — Pandit and Muslim. The former is elaborate and restricted to households. Most restaurants follow the Muslim style of cooking. Beef and pork are strictly prohibited in Srinagar to honour the religious laws of the Muslim and Hindu religions.

Most of the five-star hotels have multi-cuisine restaurants. Residency Road has some fine restaurants as well as fast food places. **Ahdoos** (tel. 72593), which is operating temporarily from a makeshift arrangement, is a popular place for Kashmiri cuisine. Try Gushtaba (goat meatballs prepared the Kashmiri way) at Rs 20 a dish. Kashmiri Pullav (with saffron) at Rs 25 is excellent.

Badaam Pasand (meat with almonds) at Rs 21 is another favourite. Ahdoos also has a lot of barbecue preparations. The food is good, though the service is very slow.

Generally, Kashmiri food is very oily, though not terribly spicy compared to food in the rest of India. A traditional Kashmiri feast is a unique event. Everybody sits on the floor in a circle and a series of thirty to forty dishes start circulating. You're meant to take a spoonful of each. Do not (as I once did out of ignorance) take vast helpings of a few, leaving half the circle glaring because that dish empties midway.

Sherwani Road, off Residency Road, has a number of eating places. **Hollywood** (tel. 75606) is a restaurant and bakery. (Srinagar has an incredible number of bakeries everywhere.) **Anarkali Fast Food** on Sherwani Road has a limited menu, but you can have good hamburgers there. The place commands a superb view of the distant snow-clad peaks. Close to Anarkali is a **Dimple's** ice cream and milk shake parlour, one of a chain in Srinagar. **Yaar's Vegetarian Restaurant** adjacent to India Coffee House, also on Sherwani Road, serves only Indian vegetarian food. A *yaar* means a 'pal', so presumably this is meant to be a friendly sort of place.

Mughal Darbar, next to Mahatta & Co. (a well-known photo shop), is a quiet little place reputed for its excellent Mughali food. The **TRC** has two restaurants, both very ordinary and with limited menus.

Along the Boulevard is the **Lhasa Restaurant,** known for excellent Chinese and Tibetan food. Tibetan food is akin to Chinese food, though with a more spicy and robust flavour. The **Coins** vegetarian restaurant, **Jheel-a-Dal** vegetarian restaurant and **Noori** are also along the Dal. The **Kashmir Darbar** in the Boulevard serves only Kashmiri non-vegetarian *wazwan* food. A *wazwan* is an elaborate traditional Kashmiri meal prepared by a master chef called a *waza*. The rituals of eating are often more elaborate than the menu itself.

Opposite the GPO, about ten minutes' walk from the TRC, is the **Tao Garden Cafe,** an open-air restaurant very popular with foreign tourists. The atmosphere is informal and relaxed, and this is an excellent meeting ground for tourists. Drop in for a drink or a snack.

LEAVING INDIA

You'll return to Delhi to catch your international flight home.
Just as you arrived in India at an ungodly hour, you'll discover
that all international flights, in a rare display of consistency, also
leave India at equally ungodly hours.

You'll therefore have some time to try and put together your
thoughts about your Indian experience: awesome monuments,
great works of art, diverse cultures, as well as annoying delays,
great poverty contrasting with affluence, an incredible past on
which a rich future is being built.

Though it's hard to try and justify those irritating and usually
quite easily avoidable problems that may have occurred during
your trip, do remember that many are manifestations of India's
remarkable democracy. Almost everyone agrees that India would
be richer, more efficient, far less problem-prone if it were run as
a totalitarian state. But it has resisted that easy solution in favour
of the far more tortuous road of democracy.

It has free and fair elections (nearly 300 million people vote in
the national elections), a highly cantankerous press, the right to
form unions and strike, and every conceivable freedom. This is
not always used wisely and responsibly, and petty tyrants can still
be obstructive, but it's an inevitable part of the growth and
maturity of the most vast experiment in democracy the world has
seen.

Farewell Advice

Your taxi will take about 45 minutes to the airport. Plan to arrive
about two hours before departure. Tell the taxi driver to take you
to the International Departure (Terminal 2) of Indira Gandhi
International Airport, which until recently was called Palam
Airport. You'll need to pay Rs 100 (£4) airport tax. Once you've
cleared passport control, you'll be through to the duty-free area
where you can browse through the goods, gazing with amused
scorn at the transit passengers feverishly buying stuff so
manifestly inferior to your magnificent acquisitions.

You are now a fully-fledged member of that travelling elite that
has 'done India'. As you wing your way home, I bid you
Namaste.

Come back again.